BIBLE STUDY COMMENTARY
Isaiah 40-Jeremiah

Bible Study Commentary

Isaiah 40–Jeremiah

ALAN COLE

Scripture Union
130, City Road, London EC1V 2NJ

CHRISTIAN LITERATURE CRUSADE
Fort Washington, Pennsylvania 19034

General Introduction

The world-wide church in the last quarter of the twentieth century faces a number of challenges. In some places the church is growing rapidly and the pressing need is for an adequately trained leadership. Some Christians face persecution and need support and encouragement while others struggle with the inroads of apathy and secularism. We must come to terms, too, with the challenges presented by Marxism, Humanism, a belief that 'science' can conquer all the ills of mankind, and a whole range of Eastern religions and modern sects. If we are to make anything of this confused and confusing world it demands a faith which is solidly biblical.

Individual Christians, too, in their personal lives face a whole range of different needs – emotional, physical, psychological, mental. As we think more and more about our relationships with one another in the body of Christ and as we explore our various ministries in that body, as we discover new dimensions in worship and as we work at what it means to embody Christ in a fallen world we need a solid base. And that base can only come through a relationship with Jesus Christ which is firmly founded on biblical truth.

The Bible, however, is not a magical book. It is not enough to say, 'I believe', and quote a few texts selected at random. We must be prepared to work with the text until our whole outlook is moulded by it. We must be ready to question our existing position and ask the true meaning of the word for us in our situation. All this demands careful study not only of the text but also of its background and of our culture. Above all it demands prayerful and expectant looking to the Spirit of God to bring the word home creatively to our own hearts and lives.

This new series of books has been commissioned in response to the repeated requests for something new to follow on from Bible Characters and Doctrines. It is now over ten years since the first series of Bible Study Books was produced and it is hoped they will reflect the changes of the last ten years and bring the Bible text to life for a new generation of readers. The series has three aims:

1. To encourage regular, systematic personal Bible reading. Each volume is divided into sections ideally suited to daily use, and will normally provide material for three months (the exceptions being Psalms and 2 Corinthians-Galatians, four months, and Mark and Ezra-Job, two months). Used in this way the books will cover the entire Bible in five years. The comments aim to give background information and enlarge on the meaning of the text, with special reference to the contemporary relevance. Detailed questions of application are, however, often left to the reader. The questions for further study are designed to aid in this respect, but are not intended to be fully comprehensive. Prayerful thought will reveal other questions for thought and areas for application. On the other hand, if you do not have time to consider all the questions select those you consider most appropriate. It is suggested that you keep a permanent record of your findings in a small notebook.

2. To provide a resource manual for group study. These books do

not provide a detailed plan for week by week study. Nor do they present a group leader with a complete set of ready-made questions or activity ideas. They do, however, provide the basic biblical material and, in the questions at the foot of each section, they give starting points for group discussion.

3. To build into a complete Bible commentary. There is, of course, no shortage of commentaries. Here, however, we have a difference. Rather than look at the text verse by verse the writers examine larger blocks of text, preserving the natural flow of the original thought and observing natural breaks.

Writers have based their comments on the Revised Standard Version and some have also used the New International Version in some detail. The books can, however, be used with any version.

Isaiah 40–66: Introduction

These chapters breathe a totally different atmosphere from the previous chapters, with their burden of Israel's sin and coming judgement. Even when the gloom lightens in chapter 38, with the story of the healing of Hezekiah from his sickness, and the promise of deliverance from Assyria, the darkness settles down again in chapter 39, with the news of the coming captivity in Babylon. So it is fitting that the chapters from 40 onwards (sometimes called *The Book of Comfort*) talk no more of judgement (so much of which has fallen already) but only of forgiveness and comfort – and ultimately, of deliverance from Babylon. For now the thought is not of beleaguered Jerusalem, capital of a tiny 'rump state': the thought is of the great world empires beyond, and God's control of them. Assyria is not the great enemy now: it is proud Babylon. Jerusalem is graphically portrayed as in ruins, and her people in exile. Yet God will call a new empire into existence to rectify the balance of the old. At first, vague references are made to 'one from the north' (41:25), and finally Cyrus the Persian is mentioned by name (45:1) as God's agent to overthrow proud Babylon, release God's people, restore the exiles, and rebuild Jerusalem. All this goes along with mockery of Babylon's great sin, idolatry (44:9–20). Woven in and through this is the new picture of God's mysterious 'servant' (42:1–9), finding a climax in chapter 53, whose true meaning cannot be seen until the days of the New Testament. The closing chapters (56–66), amid many wonderful promises, return afresh to the practical problems of the struggling community, concluding with the awful example of 66:24. But Christ, in his sermon at the synagogue of Nazareth (Luke 4:18,19), quoted 61:1,2; and in his solemn words of warning to his own disciples (Mark 9:48) he quoted 66:24, so that we dare not ignore the message of these chapters.

Isaiah 40–66: Contents

40 The book of comfort

Several books of the Old Testament can be divided into 'warning' and 'consolation'; the book of Isaiah is no exception. Until now, God's judgements have been proclaimed to Israel: from now on, God's consolation will be preached to her. Once God's judgement has fallen, there is no more wrath. If God has struck and wounded his people, he will also bind up the wounds (Hos. 6:1): Israel has suffered already a double punishment for her sins (2) as demanded under the Law (Exod. 22:4). That, for the Christian, is the meaning of the cross: since Christ has borne the punishment, there is nothing but comfort for us (Rom. 5:9). That is why the joyful cry can be raised to prepare a road for Yahweh in the desert (3) along which he may lead his ransomed people, as he had done in the days of the exodus (Exod. 13:18). In turn, the New Testament sees this as fulfilled in the message of John the Baptist, who prepared the way for Christ (Matt. 3:3).

But how can Israel be sure of this wonderful news of forgiveness? Men are so fleeting and fallible (6); is God the same? No: God's word is sure and to be trusted: it stands for ever (8). As Christ says, heaven and earth will pass away, but not his words (Mark 13:31). So it is that Israel (and we) now have a gospel to preach (9): the Good Shepherd is again lovingly leading his people (11).

Only one more question remains: granted that God loves us, granted that he promises to do these things – has he the power and ability to do them? The answer is simple: how should he not, if he is the Creator (12)? Israel knew and believed the creation story: but sometimes for them, as for us, it had seemed irrelevant to their present circumstances. For much of their history the exodus had overshadowed the creation in their thought. But now, in their darkest days, although they looked forward to a 'new exodus' from Babylon (11), even this was not enough. They needed to be reminded of the might of the Creator (12–17,21–25): and so do we (2 Cor. 5:17). If this sort of a God was for them, who could be against them (Rom. 8:31)? And, if God is truly like this, what nonsense it is to make puny little images, as idolaters do (18–20)! When the strength of the strongest of men fails, God is still unwearied (28); and, in his strength, even we can be strong (31).

TO THINK ABOUT: Why is the 'new creation' so important for the Christian (2 Cor. 5:17; Gal. 6:15)? And why is it important that God's strength is made perfect in our weakness (2 Cor. 12:7–10)?

41 God's agent

God controls international events, even in the case of those who do not know or acknowledge him, to bring about his will and purpose; that is the message of this chapter. The fact that God can not only do this, but also tell of it in advance, are the two pieces of evidence that God adduces in an imaginary law court, where he calls the peoples of the earth to confess his power (1). An unknown princeling from the East will overthrow his great Median overlord (2), overrun the Lydian empire, the richest and most feared power of Asia Minor, and take tribute even from the turbulent Greek islands and Mediterranean coastlands (5). All this the as yet unnamed warrior will do, because God has called and strengthened him (2,4). Therefore any human resistance to God is vain (41:6,7).

These soul-shattering acts of God on the world stage of history, although they may terrify the nations, bring only joy, not fear to Israel, God's people (10). Her enemies will melt away (11–13). Israel may only be a worm in men's eyes (14), the weakest, most helpless and despised of all living creatures (Ps. 22:6), but God will make her a mighty weapon in his hand (15,16).

But what if God does deliver his people from their enemies? Can he lead them home again afterwards through the desert as once he had led their ancestors through the wilderness? What will they do for water, for instance? The promises of God come tumbling out (17–20): water, shade, refreshment – all that Israel needs will be supplied abundantly and miraculously, so that the desert will be like irrigated garden-beds. All this will be so that men can see, and realise with awe, that God has done it (20). How can any idol compare with this (23,24)? Idols have no knowledge of the future, and no power to bring it about (22,23): God has both. God showed it by his foretelling of the rise of Cyrus from the north-east (25) and by sending him out on his victorious campaign. That is why God can send evangelists to Zion, bringing the good news of the coming salvation (27): no empty idol can do this.

TO THINK ABOUT: Does the Bible teach that God still controls the events of 'secular history'? If so, what are his purposes? Shall we always see and understand them now, or must we sometimes accept them in faith? If so, why?

42 The servant of Yahweh: first servant song

This is the first of what are called the 'Servant songs', a group of four or five passages in this half of Isaiah. Although separated by other chapters, these songs all hang together, and present a growing but unified picture, culminating in the great song of chapters 52 and 53. Ever since New Testament times, these songs have been seen as 'fulfilled', given their deepest and fullest meaning, in the life and death and resurrection of Jesus the Messiah (Acts 8:34,35); that is to say, they are 'prophetic', as indeed is much of the Old Testament. Such 'prophetic' passages sometimes had a partial fulfilment or fulfilments, either at the time or soon afterwards, but their full meaning will only be seen in the light of the cross and resurrection. Sometimes we can see what this partial fulfilment was; sometimes it is now lost to us, because of an ignorance of the history of the times. This is anyway unimportant, since such partial fulfilments pale into insignificance compared with the ultimate fulfilment in Christ.

Nevertheless, if we can say anything about these partial fulfilments in these notes, we will, for interest's sake, since the partial fulfilment is a 'type' or picture, imperfect though it be, of the coming Christ. For instance, in this passage the 'servant' cannot be quite the same as in 41:8,9 where 'Israel' or 'Jacob' is called God's servant – unless what is meant here is a future ideal Israel. This servant will have God's Spirit (1). He will act quietly, gently, unobtrusively (2), and he will bring justice to all the heathen nations, even the distant islands and coastlands of the Mediterranean (4). This servant is to be in himself a covenant for Israel, and a light for the heathen nations (6), to open the eyes of the blind and to free the captives (7).

These were some of the very things that Jesus claimed to be doing in his famous Nazareth sermon (Luke 4:16–21). All this is triumphantly foretold by God (7) so that we can be assured of his Godhead when these things happen. No wonder that a great hymn of praise rises from the furthest nations (10–17), marred only by the Lord's surprise at the blindness of his own people (18–23). They should have realised that even their suffering was under the control of God (24,25): and so showed his power.

TO THINK ABOUT: Is God concerned about justice for the world? If so, why? Should we be concerned? Why is it that heathen nations are more responsive to God than his own people? Why is God's prediction of his future activities so important in the Bible?

43:1–21 The ransom of Israel

God is not only the creator (1), he is also the ransomer, the redeemer.
Israel had experienced this in the past: God had 'ransomed' her from
Egypt (3). This does not only mean that God had saved her from
Egypt. It means that, in order to have Israel as his chosen people, God
gave up far mightier and wealthier peoples, like Egypt, Cush and Seba,
all or any of whom he could have chosen instead of her. That was the
price that God paid to ransom Israel.

If God had led ransomed Israel safely through the Red Sea and
Jordan (2) why should they fear for the future (Rom. 8:31,32)? Daniel's
friends would learn that God could lead safely through fire (Dan. 3:27).
What further guarantee of God's love did Israel need? True, their needs
were now different. Israel's survivors were scattered far and wide (6)
and mighty Babylon, the heart of the Chaldean empire, held them
imprisoned (14). But the God who had acted before to ransom Israel
would act again. God would bring the exiles home (6,7). God would
send his army against Babylon to overthrow it (14). How can it be that
Israel, created to be God's servant (10) so that all men may come to
know God through her, is so blind and deaf to God's lessons for her
in history (8)?

This blindness and deafness of God's people is a constant theme in
the book (compare 42:19), so God reminds them again of his power to
deliver shown at the exodus (16,17). But they must not dwell too long
on the past (18). God foretells a new thing that he is going to do, far
more wonderful than the old exodus (19). He is going to bring his
exiled people back to their land all the way from Babylon. Just as, in
the old days, he had led Israel through the wilderness of Sinai giving
them water in their need (Exod. 17:6), so now he would do the same
again (20), making even the desert birds and animals glad. Of course,
the weary columns of returning Israelite exiles would not be plodding
across a sandy desert. Their caravans would move slowly around the
'Fertile Crescent', perhaps on some of the new military 'highways' for
which the Persians were famous (19). But God's protection and provision would still be needed, and still be found (20), so that God's
people could praise him (21).

TO THINK ABOUT: In what sense is Christ's blood a ransom for us
(Mark 10:45)? At what cost (1 Pet. 1:18,19)? What should be our reaction to this? What guarantee does this give us of future provision
for our needs? What is God's ultimate aim in doing this?

There is still a problem for the sensitive soul: will God really work salvation for a people as sinful as Israel? Does God really know how unworthy of ransom they are? Yes, God does know: Israel had never truly prayed to him (22), never really sacrificed to him (23). God had always been burdened by their sins, ever since the time of Jacob their earliest ancestor (or perhaps even Adam, 27). It was because of this sin that they had been sent into exile (28). But God is the God who forgives sin (25) and Israel is still his chosen servant (44:2): God will not only forgive but also pour out his Spirit upon them (3) like water in the desert, and they will flourish like plants by irrigation channels (4). Where else is there a God like this, who first foretells and then carries out such mighty acts (8)? Certainly not with the foolish and lifeless idols of Babylon. We can imagine the Israelite exiles, in spite of their anguish of spirit, laughing at the ridiculous picture (9–20), one of several places in the book where man-made idols are mocked with rollicking peasant humour. How foolish of man to think that what he himself has made can save him: if he thinks that, it only shows how deluded he is (20).

So all heaven and earth can rejoice in God's salvation of Israel (23). If God had power enough to create the universe (24) and to make the wisest of heathen fortune-tellers look foolish (25), then his word sent through his servant will be fulfilled (26). God need only command Jerusalem and the towns of Judah to be rebuilt (26), just as he created all things in Genesis by the word of his command (Gen. 1:3; Heb. 1:3), and it will be so, just as it was in the days of the first creation (Gen. 1:7–31).

God's word always comes with power. He had proved this long ago for Israel by turning back, before their eyes, the waters of the Red Sea (Exod. 14:26–30) and of the River Jordan (Josh. 3:15–17). But now God will do it, not by his control over nature, but by his control over history; he will act not only in the 'spiritual' realm, but in the 'physical' realm as well. Tomorrow's passage will launch straight into this topic.

TO THINK ABOUT: Does salvation depend in any way upon our worthiness? If not, how can it be morally fair? In our modern society, what corresponds to the 'idols' of Old Testament days? Is our trust in technology equally naive? What is the place of joy in the Christian life?

44:28–45:13 Cyrus, God's agent

God normally uses some human agent to carry out his will. Usually it is someone unexpected, often despised and overlooked – the stone that the builders rejected proves to be the cornerstone after all (Ps. 118:22). Nowhere will this be more true than in the case of Jesus the Messiah (Matt. 21:42); but here we see it in Cyrus, the hitherto unknown prince of a minor tribe in the great Median Empire, named here as God's 'shepherd' (28) and God's 'anointed' (45:1) though not, curiously enough, God's 'servant'. That title is kept either for Israel as a whole or the mysterious servant of the Lord.

It is unusually bold, in scriptural prophecy of this sort, to name the person involved, but it is because Cyrus has a special task at a point of history. It is God's purpose to rebuild both the city of Jerusalem and the Temple, and it is Cyrus whom God will use as his agent to bring it about. That must have seemed staggering and impossible to the people of the time. As we look back on history, we can see how this all came about: for in Cyrus' first regnal year he issued his famous decree which allowed Israel to return, and commanded the rebuilding of the Temple (2 Chron. 36:23).

But how was Cyrus, a minor chieftain, to do all this? Because he was God's anointed, he would conquer all his foes (45:1). First the Median confederacy would fall: then the rich Lydia (2,3). Why did God do it for a foreigner like Cyrus who did not even know or worship Yahweh (4,5)? God did it, first, for Israel's sake (4) and secondly, so that men all over the earth should realise God's power (6). Had God not acted on a world scale, it would have remained a purely 'local' salvation. Had God the right and power to do this? Of course: God is the potter, we are the clay (9–11). That is why it was so certain that Cyrus would lead the exiles back, and rebuild Jerusalem (13), for no mortal man can stand in the way of God.

Everything now depended on the faithfulness of God to his word. If Cyrus had failed, God would have been discredited; but the whole later history of the Bible shows that God's word never falls ineffectually to the ground (Isa. 55:11).

Note: Cyrus was a monotheist, worshipping the God of heaven (Ezra 1:2) with whom he may have identified Yahweh.

TO THINK ABOUT: Why did God use a heathen king to bring about his purpose? In what sense, if any, did Cyrus' victories help men all over the known world to know the greatness of Yahweh? How does Paul use the simile of the Divine Potter (Rom. 9:19–24)?

45:14–46:13 God of the whole earth

If puny Israel is identified with such a saviour appointed by God (even if only an earthly saviour like Cyrus) she too shares in the saviour's triumph (14). The narrow vision of Israel alone worshipping the true God is now obsolete. Men will come from the ends of the human world: Egypt, Cush, Seba – even Israel's enemies will come bearing gifts to bow down and acknowledge Israel's God (14). At last the promise given to Abraham, of blessing to the Gentiles (Gen. 12:3), will be fulfilled. No doubt part of the fulfilment will be in the stream of Gentile proselytes joining the Jewish church; the great fulfilment, however, will be in Gentile Christianity. God had been hidden from them in the past (15), although not from Israel, his own people (19). But now, if the nations are wise, they can see him for themselves in his mighty acts, in the way that he controls world history and specifically by raising up Cyrus to do his will.

The tragedy is that, like those whom Paul describes in the New Testament (2 Cor. 4:4), they will not and cannot see God. Their idolatry has made them foolish (20) and they do not remember that God had foretold this action beforehand, thus showing that it was no mere coincidence but deliberately planned (21). This should be ample evidence that God is unequalled and unrivalled (21). The very farthest corners of the earth are invited to turn to him for salvation (22), though one day, willing or unwilling, they will be compelled to bow before him in surrender (23). This verse is caught up by Paul as a prophecy of the final triumph of Christ (Phil. 2:10).

What does this mean in practical terms? It means that mighty Bel and Nebo, highest gods of Babylon, will go into exile in their turn as captives, as once Israel had done. The idols will go bumping off in saddlebags on animals' backs (46:1), while it is God himself who will carry Israel in triumph, as he has always done (3). But what if Israel is now old and feeble, not as she was in earlier days? God will still carry her, even in old age and weakness (4). What can man-made idols do to compare with this (5–7)? Costly they may well be (6) but they are lifeless and powerless objects (7). God is the one who both foretold Cyrus' coming, and raised him up like an eagle, coming from the far east (10,11), so accomplishment of his purpose is sure (13). Stubborn though Israel may be, her unbelief will not impede the working of God.

47 Judgement in Babylon

There can be no salvation without judgement as well: that is the message of the cross. Salvation for Israel had meant judgement for Egypt; the return of the exiles will only be made possible after the fall of Babylon to the Persians. Babylon is here personified as a proud queen, brought down from her throne (1) to do the lowest slaves' work (2), grinding meal at the mill, openly shamed before all (3).

Why does God judge Babylon so harshly? Because of her pride and sinful luxury and haughtiness (5)? No doubt, but there is a deeper reason here, which is often enunciated in the Old Testament. God uses heathen nations to punish his sinful people (6) just as he will use a heathen nation to bring his people back to Zion: that was often a stumbling-block to the pious then, as it is today. But God will hold that heathen nation to account for the way that she used or abused the power given her (6). If she used her position cruelly or proudly, the very judge will be judged (6,7). So Assyria had fallen; so too would Babylon the Great fall. She was self-satisfied and self-confident. She could not believe that disaster would ever overtake her (8,9) but it did, because she had not laid to heart God's judgement on Israel, of which she had been the agent.

It was not as though Babylon had no defences. If we today have the great god Science to protect us, she had Magic (9). That may seem futile to us, but no one in the ancient world would have seen it in that way. Babylonian astrologers were famous, and justly so: they had made many true astronomical observations and discoveries. But astronomy had fallen into a morass of superstition. Casting horoscopes and predicting the future had become a major preoccupation, with endless tables and weary calculations (12,13). All this misdirected toil and bogus science was useless, for it was totally unable to save Babylon from the coming disaster (11). Neither astrology nor the Babylonian star-gods would help them. The whole system is compared to a pile of dry straw, going up in a blaze (14). There is a grim irony in the description: this is no domestic fire for cooking or heat, for 'our God is a consuming fire' (Heb. 12:29). And what of the highly-trained astrologers, when the blow falls on Babylon? They will flee for their lives in every direction (15), powerless to help, thinking only of themselves.

TO THINK ABOUT: If bogus science could not save Babylon, can real science save us? Why are so many people turning back to astrology and horoscopes today? Is this harmless or serious? Why does the Christian reject it?

48 God's word to Israel

Once again, although God speaks words of comfort to Israel, he is under no illusions about Israel's true nature. He knows their hypocrisy and obstinacy, their refusal to respond to him (1,4). But he did not reject them because of this; instead, he redoubled his efforts to make them understand. For instance, had the event of salvation happened with no advance warning, they would have given the credit for it to their idols (5) – as we might put an event down to 'science' or 'natural causes' today. So, long before he acted, God had revealed his purposes (3) so that when they happened people would have to admit that it was truly God's activity. But wilful Israel had deliberately misunderstood even this. She treated the event, when it happened, as 'stale news' – she had heard of it long ago, so it was nothing new or wonderful in her eyes. So now God in his mercy would use yet another way: he would reveal new things to them, things just about to happen, of which they had never heard before (6,7). Presumably the rise of Cyrus within the next few years was one such event. Would this make rebellious Israel listen (8)?

As often in the Mosaic story, God was acting like this 'for the sake of his name' (9). This, in the Bible, means 'because of his nature': it is not merely God's reputation that is at stake. Otherwise his anger would have blazed out and he would have destroyed Israel: as it was, he sent 'his chosen' (Cyrus) to carry out his will in judgement on Babylon (14). If only Israel had listened to the message of God before, what happiness could have been hers (18). But even now God's grace will triumph: Israel can escape from Babylon with joy (20) as Israel had from Egypt long ago. Like Israel of old they would not lack anything on the journey home (21): it is only for the wicked, those who reject God, that there is no happiness (22).

TO THINK ABOUT: Is God surprised when we fall into sin, or only grieved? Does he realise how bad the Christian church actually is? If so, why does he go on using it? Why are humans so obstinately blind to God's activity? In this chapter, is God promising to meet all the physical needs of the returning exiles? Does he promise to meet ours in the same way?

49:1–50:3 Second servant song

Now we come to the second of the so-called 'Servant songs'. Although they are often isolated for study, they cannot be easily detached from their context. Some scholars say that this song comprises only verses 1 to 6, while others include verses 7, 8 and 9 in it. But the whole of the rest of the chapter is actually a commentary on and explanation of these first few verses. However, the title is convenient, summing up, as it does, the main object of the passage.

Who is this servant? Of course, on the basis of the New Testament, we can say that ultimately, in prophetic fulfilment, the servant is Christ: when the Ethiopian eunuch asked this question long ago (Acts 8:34) this is certainly the answer that Philip gave (Acts 8:35). But in the immediate sense, who was he? He is described as 'Israel' (3), but yet his task is to bring back wayward Israel to God (5). We can only assume that he is therefore some individual, representing 'ideal Israel'. This sense of individuality is borne out by the numerous occurrences of 'me' 'my' and 'I' in the English translation (1–5), while Yahweh addresses the servant directly as 'you' (6). God has called him from before birth (1,5) as he had called Jeremiah (Jer. 1:5). The servant's task was to bring to Israel God's messages, sharp as any sword or arrow (2). The servant had thought his work a total failure (4), but God had vindicated him. Now God has revealed an even greater task to the servant: it is not just to bring back the scattered exiles of Israel, but to be 'a light for the Gentiles' till God's salvation reaches to the ends of the earth (6). Yes, even kings and leaders will, at the last, honour God's servant whom once they had despised (7). The servant will be in his own person a covenant given by God to his people (8).

This 'covenant' will involve freedom and release for God's people (9), as the old covenant had for Israel in Exodus days. They will journey home safely (10) as Israel did, untouched by desert hardships (10). Did Israel really think that God had forgotten her? No: that was impossible even on human arguments (14–16). The closing verses reiterate the marvels of their return (18–26), and the unchanging nature of God's love (50:1). God has not divorced Israel, his bride; so of course he will use his power to deliver her.

50:4 –11 Third servant song

In this song, we have come still further along the road of God's revelation. The servant is now more clearly an individual than ever before, and speaks in the first person at last. He calls himself a 'learner', a disciple of God's (4,5): he spends time each morning listening to the voice of God, so that he may speak and encourage the weary (4). The Christian will think at once of Jesus rising 'a great while before day' (Mark 1:35) for communion with God. But now the servant is not merely scorned by others as before: he is persecuted and insulted, with blows and spitting (6). Yet in all this suffering, he neither resists nor attempts to escape: he meekly turns the other cheek (6). Such meek behaviour is almost unknown in the Old Testament, where 'an eye for an eye' is the normal rule (Exod. 21:24). Only isolated men like Jeremiah had suffered like this. To us, the parallel of the behaviour of Jesus at his trial becomes more clear (1 Pet. 2:23), a picture which will be even clearer in the last servant song.

How then does the suffering servant endure such injustice so patiently? Because of Yahweh's help (7) he can endure anything: he knows that, at the last, he will not be shamed. He knows that he will be vindicated before Yahweh, while his accusers will vanish away (9). In the light of that coming vindication by God, he can endure the present.

What is the practical value of this for Israelite exiles who are suffering persecution for their faith, men like Daniel and his friends (Dan. 3:12)? If they listen to what God's servant says, they too will have hope, even though they walk in darkness now (10). This 'darkness' may refer also to the Gentiles who hear the servant. Not only the Israelites who already 'fear Yahweh' but those Gentiles who are still in darkness without him can learn, from the servant's words and example, to trust in Yahweh. But those who do not trust him, those who do not walk the path of the servant, are 'playing with fire'. Ultimately the very fire that they have kindled will consume them. This is a common Old Testament metaphor, used in a land where bush fires were so frequent (Exod. 3:2; 1 Kings 19:12). The irony of this sort of judgement is that men have made it for themselves.

TO THINK ABOUT: Why is it necessary for God's servants to spend time regularly alone with God? Is God's ultimate punishment to leave people to themselves? Why is this the worst that can happen to a person?

51:1–16 Look back

If Israel is called, in her extremity, to remember the creation story, she is also called to remember her ancestors Abraham and Sarah, summoned by God to be a nation when their numbers were far smaller than those of exiled Israel (1,2), and yet multiplied by God's blessing. She is also advised to remember Eden, the paradise of God. God can turn the war-ravaged lands of Israel into another Eden (3); no wonder that Israel's heart will be full of joy (3) as in Psalm 126:2.

But how will God achieve this miracle? He will introduce his salvation by a universal world judgement, for there is no salvation without judgement. God will issue his decree (4) and 'judge' the nations, remembering that in the Bible 'to judge' means to right the wrongs of the helpless and down-trodden as well as to punish the wicked and the oppressors. 'Judge' therefore means much the same as 'save', to the weak. Heaven and earth will flee away in terror at God's coming (6). Earth's inhabitants will die like flies; but God's salvation will endure for ever. This may be the doomsday syndrome; but those who have God's laws in their hearts have nothing to fear (7). As the New Testament will say, they can lift up their heads, knowing that their redemption is near (Luke 21:28). Their enemies will 'melt away' (8).

Such a judgement and such a deliverance are not to be attained without the winning of the 'last battle'. But if, in poetic Hebrew imagery, God had already fought and conquered the dragons of the deep (9) in bringing order out of chaos at the creation, could he not win the same battle again? Sometimes Rahab and the dragon stand for spiritual forces conquered by God: sometimes they stand for physical world-powers like Egypt, overthrown by God in order to free his people. The direct reference to the crossing of the Red Sea suggests the latter meaning here (10). No wonder that the exiles will return to Jerusalem joyfully (11). If they are at present afraid of their oppressors, it is only because they have forgotten the might of God (13,15). He, in all his might, is the one who has made Israel his own people and the bearers of his message to mankind (16). Could grace go further?

TO THINK ABOUT: What other reasons made it appropriate for Israel, in Babylon, to remember Abraham? Why should Israel remember Eden? Does the possible destruction of the universe terrify the Christian? If not, why not? What gives the Christian permanence? Is Satan already conquered, or is Christ's victory still to come?

51:17–52:12 Jerusalem, awake!

If the day of God's salvation really is dawning, then Israel must bestir herself, to be ready to respond. When the great moment of deliverance comes, she must be as ready to leave Babylon as her ancestors had been to leave Egypt (Exod. 12:11). As it is, she is helpless and hopeless, 'punch-drunk' and reeling under God's judgement (17). Remorselessly, God reminds her of the awfulness and completeness of that judgement (18–20). But when she has seen and realised all this, and realised too that the blow has fallen upon her from the Lord, he has a deeper and more wonderful message. The cup of suffering (22) is to be taken from Israel's hand, and put by God into the hand of her tormentors instead (23). Now, then, is the time for Jerusalem to shake off her prisoners chains, rise from the dust and put on her finest garments (52:1,2) like the prodigal son on his return home (Luke 15:22). How can this be? It is because, unlike other slaves and war-captives, she had not been sold by God for money (3). Babylon had no rights over her. She remained God's property, God's people, and he owes no man anything when he takes her back. He is only vindicating his name before his people (6).

Now the picture moves to the 'evangelists', the messengers running over the mountains to bring to Jerusalem the good news of God's deliverance of his people (7). Perhaps it is the good news of the rise of Cyrus, of his decree of liberation (2 Chron. 36:23) and of the imminent return to Israel of the captives. The watchmen at Jerusalem answer back (8) and both groups together sing for joy at what God has done for his chastened people.

There is, however, one demand on God's redeemed nation: she must be utterly different and separate from all other people of the earth. This is not something new; it had been already demanded under the Law (Deut. 23:3). It is expressed in two ways: the new Jerusalem must be free from 'the uncircumcised' (non-Jewish people) and 'the unclean' (52:1). The tragedy of later Israel was that she would interpret this in a physical and ritualistic sense only. The second way of expressing their distinctiveness was to be the readiness of the exiles to leave unclean Babylon at God's call, especially those who were to carry home the Temple vessels (11) as recorded in Ezra 1:8–10.

TO THINK ABOUT: Why is the wine cup in the Bible the symbol of suffering (Mark 10:38) as well as of joy? Why was physical separation from Gentile peoples demanded of Israel (Deut. 29:16–18)? What is the corresponding Christian principle today? What 'gospel' was there to preach in Old Testament days? Was it nationalistic? What is the difference today?

52:13–53:12 Fourth servant song

This is the very heart of the servant songs (the exact number of which depends upon how they are divided up). There is no question here as to the individuality of the servant: the only question raised is as to his exact identity – and that is no mystery for the Christian.

The main theme of the song will be the suffering and rejection of the servant, but it begins with a strong statement of his ultimate triumph and exaltation (13) lest we should be crushed by his humiliation. True, his appearance will show such marks of suffering that he will seem hardly human (14). Heathen rulers will be utterly dumbfounded, presumably not only at the extent of his sufferings, but at his subsequent triumph (15). How could they have guessed any of these totally unforeseen things?

That indeed is the theme of chapter 53 – the unexpected and unbelievable nature of the work of God (1) even when we hear the incredible news. The servant came from unlikely origins, and no special outward qualities of attractiveness made him naturally appealing (2). Worse still, he was despised and forsaken by his fellow men: no one thought anything of him (3). Sorrow and sickness seemed to have dogged his life. Out of either aversion or sympathy, people would look away, to avoid seeing him.

What reason could there possibly be for this? Orthodox Hebrew theology was clear on such a point: a man like this was clearly being punished by God (4). 'Smitten by God' is often used to explain the condition of the leper; 2 Chron. 26:20, for instance. Punishment it was, says the prophet, but with a difference: it was punishment for *our* sins, not his own, that he was suffering (4–6). That is wonder enough: but a greater wonder still is the fact that the servant's suffering on our behalf brought healing and wholeness for us (5). We, in other words, are forgiven because the servant endured our punishment instead.

There are many other rich points, which can only be summarised here. The servant would suffer silently and patiently (7). But all this was fulfilling God's plan (10), so the servant's ultimate vindication and success are sure, even if it is on the other side of death (11,12).

54 Assurance of salvation

If chapter 53 is a proclamation of salvation, chapter 54 is the assurance of it. Often in the Old Testament, Israel (when under God's anger) is compared to a deserted and childless wife or widow (1). Here is another miracle: the infertile and abandoned wife will now bear so many children that the obliging Bedouin tent will have to be stretched out still further to its utmost limits to accommodate them all (2). As such a tent has no ridge pole, and any required number of tent poles may be used, this is fairly easily managed: it only needs stronger tent pegs and longer guy-ropes (2). Her present joy will be so great that all the shame of her past will be forgotten (4).

To the Hebrew, either widowhood or childlessness was a reproach (as was desertion) because they were considered a sign of God's punishment of the unfortunate women concerned (4). But now God will be truly Israel's husband again (5) and she will be like a once rejected wife, joyfully welcomed back (6). The marriage covenant between God and Israel will be established again, as in Hosea 2:16–20.

But will it last, this reconciliation experience? If Israel sins again, will God reject her again, this time for ever? No: what sort of salvation would this be, with no assurance of continuance? God's anger with Israel had been brief, but now he will show her everlasting love and mercy (8). There are parallels to this in the Old Testament. Noah's Flood was a 'once for all' example of judgement (9). God had sworn that he would never again wipe out all mankind with a similar deluge (Gen. 9:11). That indeed was his new covenant with mankind (Gen. 9:9), made because of God's full knowledge of human weakness and therefore inevitable sinfulness (Gen. 8:21). The most stable things in life may go, but not God's steadfast love for his people (10). The new Jerusalem will be built not of stones, but of jewels (11,12) – a symbolic way of describing her preciousness to God (compare Revelation 21:15–21) – and no one will be able to harm her (14). How could any weapon succeed against God's people, if it is God who creates the very blacksmiths who make them (16)? Even the world's armaments manufacturers are in the hand of God.

TO THINK ABOUT: What about the Jewish people now? Has God rejected them (Rom. 9 and 11)? Could God ever reject the Christian church? If not, why does Paul warn us to beware (Rom. 11:17–22)? Could he reject individual Christians (Heb. 10:26–31)? If not, why not? Were all these prophecies about Jerusalem fulfilled literally? If not, can we understand them of the 'new Jerusalem' (Rev. 21:2)?

55 God's invitation

Palestine is a shrewd and hard-headed country where even today water is bought and sold especially if, as in some places, it must be carried. What nonsense then is this promise of God's? Those who are hungry and thirsty, but who have no money, are nevertheless summoned by God to come and eat and drink – not merely to drink water, the necessity of life, but milk and wine, life's luxuries (1). Even more startlingly, they are told that in this topsy-turvy world they are spending what money they have on 'junk foods' that can neither nourish nor satisfy (2). This is not an ancient campaign against worthless breakfast-foods: it is a call to men and women to turn to God as the only source of true satisfaction (3). If only they do this, God will make with them the sort of covenant that he had made with David long before, when he promised never to reject David's descendants from his purposes (2 Sam. 7:16). Just as this covenant had made David a leader and witness to the non-Jewish peoples as well as to his own Israel (4), so it will be true for God's people now (5) – heathen nations will flock to join them for the sake of their God.

So the invitation to return to God is issued again: now is the opportunity to repent (6). Let there be no mistake: to turn to God always involves renunciation of known wrong and sin (7), otherwise it is only empty mockery. But will repentance achieve anything? Yes, God will have mercy and he will pardon the sinner who leaves his sin and turns to God (7). This is incredible, for no man would ever treat a sinner like this. How can we be so sure that God will do it? There are two reasons for our belief, says the prophet: the first is that, because God's thoughts are infinitely higher than ours, we should never restrict him to working in human ways (8,9). The second reason is that we have God's promise that he will indeed forgive (16,17). God's word, because it is an expression of his will, purpose, and intention to act, is seen in the Bible almost as something alive in itself (10,11). It is not magic, but it is supernatural, so God's word cannot fail (11). No wonder that all nature rejoices before such a God, and that the effects of the curse upon the earth (Gen. 3:17) will be seen no more (12,13). Instead, there will only be signs of God's blessing.

TO THINK ABOUT: Why are the metaphors of 'hunger' and 'thirst' used so often in the Bible? How does Jesus use them? Is there ever a time when we may seek repentance in vain? Why do preachers like John the Baptist insist that we should 'produce fruit in keeping with repentance' (Matt. 3:8)? Is not faith sufficient in itself?

56:1–8 What of the outsider?

There is always, in any society, an 'in-group' and an 'out-group', and Israel was no exception to this rule. As far as Israel could see, salvation was centred on her alone; there had been little as yet to say to the Gentile world outside. Perhaps many of our churches hold a similar attitude today.

There were two groups in particular who felt 'outsiders' as far as Israel was concerned: the foreigner and the eunuch (3). Some sorts of foreigner (Deut. 23:3) and all sorts of eunuch (Deut. 23:1) were totally banned from the meeting-tent, and no Gentile might enter the inner courts of the later Temple in Jerusalem. But here God announces that he will abolish all these distinctions (as he did finally in Christ, Gal. 3:28). Going further still, he has special promises and rewards for these 'second-class citizens' (4).

The anguish of the eunuch, apart from his exclusion from worship, was that, having no children, he would have no family to remember him after death: he was like a dead tree (3). But here God promises that if such people cling fast to his covenant, he will give them a place in his house, and an everlasting name better than any son or daughter (5). Some have suggested that Nehemiah, being a high official at the Persian court, may have been one such (Neh. 1:11); the Ethiopian treasurer certainly was (Acts 8:27). The foreigner's fear, even if he became a proselyte, was that God would still exclude him from his people (3). Instead, God promises him full access to his Temple at Jerusalem, and acceptance of his offerings (7). Indeed, he explains his final purpose, unguessed till now by the Hebrews: God desires his Temple to be a prayer-place not just for Israel but for all the nations (7). Instead of this, men had made God's Temple a veritable thieves' market. This is the verse quoted by Jesus, when he drove the merchants from the Temple (Mark 11:17).

Note that eunuchs were probably excluded from worship because of the existence of eunuch-priests of pagan gods. Their prohibition may also stem from the reasoning behind the rule that only perfect specimens of animals could be fittingly offered to God. The emphasis on sabbath-keeping (2), alongside justice and integrity (2), is typical of later Judaism. The sabbath was a clearly-seen outward sign of God's covenant (6), especially when living among heathen people who did not observe it. It was also an expression of faith in God's provision.

TO THINK ABOUT: Why was salvation virtually restricted to the Hebrews in Old Testament times, and why is it equally open to all mankind today? What would correspond to sabbath-keeping as a sign of God's covenant today? Why do physical debilities not rule us out from participation in Christian worship?

56:9–57:13 The reaction against God

It is a great spiritual principle that, whenever there is a spiritual move forward, there is also a counter-attack by the powers of evil: this period in Israel's history is no exception. We cannot tell whether it is to be seen against a background in Palestine, or in Babylon, for this sort of heathen worship was universal. Again, the question is not important.

First of all, the 'shepherds' are rebuked, those whom God has put in positions of responsibility: they are sheepdogs that are blind, dumb, sleepy, greedy, selfish (10,11). Alcohol is their only concern (12). If the leaders are like this, what wonder that the upright are persecuted and even killed (57:1), although this death may be for some only the gateway to peace (2)? But just because this is permitted, it does not mean that God has not seen it, nor does it mean that God will not act to avenge it. Those who persecute the righteous like this cannot be children of God (3). Jesus said of such (John 8:44) that they were children of Satan, who is the father of lies and untruth (4). They worship heathen gods of sex (5) and cruelty, for even their own first-born babies were offered up in sacrifice (5) to Baal. When the Old Testament speaks of adultery and immorality, it often means religious unfaithfulness to God, whose covenant is seen as a marriage bond with Israel. But, since Baal-worship was associated with sexual licence, the metaphorical often passes into the literal (7,8). Bad theology makes bad morals: that is the message of the Old Testament. The breakdown of the moral fabric of the Western world, following its abandonment of Christian faith, is an obvious modern illustration, but so was the break-up of the Israelite kingdom, consequent on its abandonment of God's covenant.

Yet God's rebuke is not so much stern as plaintive: how could they expect such behaviour to please him (6)? Of whom were they afraid, that they should reject their own God, and refuse him a place in their heart (11)? But there comes a time when even the loving patience of God himself is exhausted. He will show to all men what his people are really like. When disaster comes, when God's judgement falls, let their idols save them – if they can (13). Too late: they will be gone with the wind; the only safety lies in trust in God.

57:14 –21 The recipients of God's salvation

Is there any hope for God's people if they are as sinful as described? Yes; God still promises salvation for them (14), even though he is so holy and so far removed from sin (15). But there is only one type of mortal who can endure the presence of such a God: it is the humble and contrite (15). Humility is one of the greatest virtues in the Bible, as pride is one of the greatest sins: perhaps because humility predisposes us to faith, while pride utterly excludes us from it. That is why God 'resists the proud but gives grace to the humble' (Jas. 4:6); that is why, as here, he punishes the proud. But God's punishment is what Hebrews would call 'disciplining' (Heb. 12:5): it is only designed to produce in mankind that humbled spirit, the broken and contrite heart (Ps. 51:17), that will be accepted by God. How can we be sure that this is God's final purpose, and that he does not punish merely in order to destroy? He knows the weakness of mankind whom he has made (Ps. 103:14). As in Genesis 6:3, God is moved to pity by the very frailty of his own creation (16).

True, God will strike in anger (17) as he had struck wayward Israel: she had chosen her own rebellious path, and must therefore suffer the consequences. But the one who struck her will also heal and comfort her (18), for the whole purpose of the punishment will have been achieved if only Israel is humbled. Now God can bring a message of peace and reconciliation (19), both to those near to God and those far away from him. This passage is interpreted in the New Testament (Acts 2:39) as covering the most distant of Gentiles as well as the Jew who is already not far from the kingdom of God (Mark 12:34). God's salvation is not limited to those who are 'nearly saved' already. But the Bible teaches us, sadly, that not all of God's chastening produces the desired results. If we accept it in the right spirit, then, unpleasant though it is at the time, it will produce the fruits of righteousness (Heb. 12:11). If we are hardened, punishment becomes destruction (Heb. 12:15–17). There is no peace, no reconciliation with God, for those who refuse him (21). They are like the restless sea, endlessly tossing flotsam on the beach.

TO THINK ABOUT: In what ways does God discipline his children today? What is his purpose in doing it? What is Christian humility? What did Jesus say about it? Why is humility unpopular in the modern world?

58 What is true religion?

When God proclaims a nation's sin (1) we usually expect a catalogue of vices, whether personal or public. But here, as so often in the prophets, it is Israel's 'religiosity' that is attacked (2). God is not opposed to religious ceremonial as such, although none is actually enjoined in the New Testament. Indeed, in the Old Testament he commands Israel to observe a most elaborate ritual system (eg. Exod. 29). But God abhors outward forms that are utterly divorced from inner spiritual reality. That is a fair picture of much of the religion of Israel in practice, and perhaps much of our modern religion too.

Israel starts in the right way, seeking God and his law of justice like a nation really wanting to act with integrity (2). True, they feel somewhat aggrieved: God somehow does not seem to notice their elaborate ritual fasts and penances as he should do (3). At their attitude, God's anger blazes out. This sort of 'fast' outlined with selfishness and oppression of others (3) can never please God (5), even though in outward detail it is rigorous.

Then comes the striking definition of the only sort of fast that does please God (6). It is to free the prisoner and the oppressed, to feed the hungry, to house the poor, to clothe the naked (6,7). The list reads like that in Matthew 25:35,36. But in what sense is this 'fasting'? In two ways: first, it is true self-denial, and will cost us dearly. Second, it is a practical way of showing genuine repentance and change of heart, as John the Baptist showed his disciples (Matt. 3:8).

For a people who act in this way, the 'day' will dawn (8,10); when such a people prays, God will be quick to answer (11). Neither experiences of darkness (10) nor desert (11) will daunt her: God will give continual guidance and strength in the desert, as he had done in the old days of the exodus. Indeed, Israel will repair all the past ruins of the years: and from this she will take her proud new title (12). Once again for Israel, the keeping of the sabbath, sign to her of God's covenant, will be the acid test of whether she chooses what pleases God or what pleases herself (13). For those who make the right choice God's blessing is assured (14).

TO THINK ABOUT: Is it true that the Old Testament prophets are opposed to ritual? If not, what do they oppose, and why? Why are so few outward forms laid down in the New Testament? What is the relationship between 'faith' and 'works'? What does the Bible mean by 'death to self' (Rom. 6:1–14)?

59 What are God's people like?

If God fails to save Israel as he had done in the past, it is not because he has neither the knowledge of their situation nor the power to save them (1). It is because of the rift between men and God caused by human sin (2). Paul, in Romans 3:15–17, quotes some of these verses to describe not only the people of his day, but the people of every day and every place. The Christian must be realistic in his view of mankind, or the full wonder of God's redemption will never be seen. Murder, deceit, treachery: it seems to be universal (3,4). If this seems to us an extreme judgement, we should remember that Jesus taught that the thought was as bad as the deed (Matt. 5:28). When John the Baptist called the Pharisees a 'brood of vipers', he may have been thinking of this vivid metaphor of snakes' eggs (5), eggs which the Hebrews believed poisonous to eat but impossible to destroy, for breaking them only released the snake. It is thus a symbol of an evil that cannot be handled by men.

What of all their deceitful planning and scheming? It is as complex as a spider's web (5), a tissue of deceits. Unlike a silkworm's cocoon, webs woven like this are no good for clothing. Their plots are equally useless (6); all their cleverness is for nothing. The final condemnation on them is that they never have known the way of peace, the path of right relations with God and man; and nobody who follows these people will ever know peace either (8).

That is why mankind 'finds only darkness', not light (9); and why men 'grope about at midday', morally blind (10). That is why there is 'no justice or integrity in the land' (9) and why, although men keep hoping for justice, it never comes (11). At least men are now ready to acknowledge their sins to God (12), and rebellion against God is chief (13). But what will God do, faced with all this fabric of injustice? The Lord sees; the Lord is angered. Since no one else will act, he will himself (15,16). God will intervene both in judgement (18) and in salvation (20) so that, to the very ends of the earth, men will see his glory revealed. Never again will his covenant leave his servants. His spirit and his words will remain with them for ever (21).

TO THINK ABOUT: Is the human race really as bad as the Bible says? What does the Bible mean by 'peace'? What is the difference between verse 17 and 'the armour of God' in Ephesians 6:10–18?

60 The new Jerusalem

This chapter is a hymn of praise telling of the restored Jerusalem, rebuilt by God himself. She must shine in the darkness with the glory of the Lord (1) so that the nations still in darkness may flock to her light (3). We are very close now to the New Testament concept of the gospel witness of the church. Here are the nations, streaming into the city of God, bringing Jerusalem's sons and daughters, God's scattered people, home from exile (4). God is gathering together his people at last. The wealth of the nations will flow into Jerusalem, as sacrifices to God on his altar in the Temple, from far-flung Gentiles who come to worship the true God at last (6,7). This was not of course fulfilled literally at the physical Temple in Jerusalem, although many proselytes doubtless entered the Temple, as far as they were allowed to go, in the following centuries. But it was fulfilled in the Christian church, with its preaching of the gospel to the Gentiles (Eph. 2:17).

As so often in Old Testament prophecy, there is a blend of the near and distant future (as in Jesus' prophecy in Matt. 24). Foreign Persian kings did indeed give permission for the Temple to be restored (2 Chron. 36:23) and the walls of Jerusalem to be rebuilt (10). But this earthly Jerusalem never dared leave her gates open at night (Neh. 7:3); that was reserved for the heavenly Jerusalem, still to come (11). It was Nehemiah who obtained permission to hew cedars of Lebanon for walls and houses (Neh. 2:8) as prophesied in verse 13. Only rarely in this world would Israel's oppressors bow down before her (14): but one day every knee will bow to Christ (Rom. 14:11).

Many of these promises must thus be taken in a spiritual sense, and must be seen as fulfilled only in Christ. Solomon, for a few brief years, might have made gold as common as bronze in Israel (17), but no Israelite ruler would ever do it again. Instead, God would send to Jerusalem those rarest of all commodities – peace, salvation, praise (17,18). No need for sun and moon to shine for those who already have God for their light (19), although the sun and moon still rise and set every day above the earthly Jerusalem. At the deepest level, this is only finally true of the heavenly Jerusalem (Rev. 21:23). But, a miracle greater than any of these, Israel will be changed in heart: at last she will be upright (21) and God will be glorified.

TO THINK ABOUT: What is 'prophecy' and what do we mean by 'fulfilment of prophecy'? Is all Old Testament prophecy to be fulfilled literally? If not, why not? What does the Bible tell us about the 'New Jerusalem?' Can we expect to see anything of it in this life?

61 God's messenger

It is not clear whether in the first place this chapter is describing the task of the prophet himself, or of the servant of whom he tells elsewhere. But again, to the Christian, this is not a significant question; for Christ, preaching in the synagogue at Nazareth, said that it was finally fulfilled in him (Luke 4:18,19).

This agent of God has been 'anointed', specially designated for his task, by the gift of God's Spirit, and his task is to bring good news to the poor and the prisoners (1). There was little good news for the poor in Old Testament days (is there any more nowadays?) and none at all for the wretched prisoners. But God will give them freedom, for this is the 'year of God's favour' (2), probably meaning the sabbatical year or the great Jubilee year of release (Exod. 21:2; Lev. 25). We know that at least once in Israel's history slaves were actually so released (Jer. 34:9). But it was apparently only done under duress, and when the danger went, the slaves were re-possessed by their old masters (Jer. 34:11), to Jeremiah's wrath (Jer. 34:17). Perhaps this sort of behaviour is why God's 'year of favour' is also described as his 'day of vengeance' (2), a clause omitted by Jesus in his Nazareth sermon (Luke 4:19).

God would do more than that: those who mourned would be comforted (3), and the ancient ruins in Israel would be rebuilt (4). Instead of serving foreigners, foreigners would now serve them (5). This 'tit for tat' was the only way, in Old Testament times, that God's justice could be seen to be vindicated on this side of the grave, as in those days it must be. At last the great promise made to Moses, that God's people would be a 'kingdom of priests' (Exod. 19:6), was to be realised (6), although the realisation would only be in the Christian church (1 Pet. 2:9).

But all this will only be because God's nature is what it is (8) and because he is willing to make an 'everlasting covenant' with them. Now at last the promise to Abraham will be fulfilled (Gen. 12:3): the very Gentiles will see and acknowledge that God has blessed Israel (9). So the prophet, speaking on behalf of Israel, lifts up his heart in exultation to God for what God has done in saving and changing his people (10). A veritable harvest of righteousness and praise is springing up before their eyes.

62 Glorious Zion

This inspired poem runs so closely with chapter 60 as to be almost a continuation of it. Some of the thoughts are therefore the same, for example, that the heathen nations will see Israel's glory (2). But there is a fresh thought here, that Jerusalem will have a 'new name' (compare with Rev. 2:17), this time given by Yahweh himself (2). After all, Jerusalem had been her old name long before she was the site of God's Temple: *Urusalimmu* is found in early cuneiform tablets. But, in the Bible, 'name' virtually means 'nature', so that a change of name like this is most significant; it means that Zion's very nature will be changed, as Jacob's nature had to be changed to make him 'Israel' (Gen. 32:28). Hosea had used the same metaphor long before when Israel, previously called 'Unloved' and 'Not-My-People', became 'Loved' and 'My People' (Hos. 2:1). Now the city once called 'Forsaken' will be called 'Delight', and her deserted land will be called 'Married' (4), for God will be her true husband: that is to say, he will keep his covenant of love for ever (5).

But meanwhile, there is a task for Zion to perform. The restoration promised by God has not yet taken place, so those whom God has placed as 'watchmen' over Jerusalem must continue earnestly in prayer until he has restored her (6,7). Every Asian king had a 'reminder' whose task was not only to record events, but to recall them if necessary to his memory. Darius the Persian had a herald, whose daily task was to say: 'Sir, remember the Athenians,' until Darius had punished them for rebellion. God has his 'remembrancers' too, those who intercede for his people, but the result is already certain (8).

This, however, does not mean that God's people have nothing to do but await God's action. On the contrary, they are exhorted to show their faith by building and repairing roads (perhaps the highways from Babylon), so that God's plan may come true (10). As Paul would say, they must work out their salvation knowing that God is also at work in them (Phil. 2:12,13). If, and as, they do this, God will act: there will be a 'triumphal entry' into Jerusalem of their saviour (11). This passage, amongst others, was quoted at the entry of Christ into the Holy City (Matt. 21:5). This final act of God will give true meaning to Israel's change of name; for the reality, symbolised by the new name, will have come at last (12).

TO THINK ABOUT: What does the passage in Revelation mean which says that each of us will have a 'new name' (Rev. 2:17)? How much does God's work depend upon our prayers? If it does, how can God be all-powerful? If it does not, why are we told to pray? In what way was Christ's triumphal entry into Jerusalem a fulfilment of this passage?

63:1–6 God's day of vengeance

This picture is a grim, but vivid, picture of God's day of vengeance on his enemies, although at the same time it is a day of vindication and salvation for his people (1,4). God is pictured moving up from Edom, to the south-east of Israel (Bozrah is an Edomite city); elsewhere in the Old Testament he is described as coming either from Teman or Paran (Hab. 3:3), areas in the 'deep south' and thus in the general vicinity of Sinai. Sometimes Sinai, Seir (Edom), and Paran are used as virtual synonyms (Deut. 33:2) because Israel, unlike other nations, did not think of their God as living in one fixed location on earth. His throne was in heaven, although he had once come down and revealed himself on Mount Sinai (Ps. 68:7,8) and had once marched at the head of his people through the wilderness (Ps. 68:7). Now he is marching north again, to deliver them as he had of old.

But there is another reason for the mention here of Edom and Bozrah (1): Edom had become a traditional picture of the Gentile enemies of God's people (Ps. 137:7). So in Isaiah, Jeremiah, and Ezekiel, God's coming judgement on Edom is foretold as a symbol of his judgement on all his enemies. In later Jewish days, 'Edom' became a code word for Rome, the hated oppressor.

The simile of the winepress of the wrath of God comes from the Palestinian custom of cutting the grape-bunches at the autumn harvest, collecting them in the winepress (often hollowed out of the solid rock) and then treading the grapes down with bare feet. Feet and clothing alike were spotted and stained with the red grape juice, like the blood stains on a soldier after battle (2). The parallel with the last great battle, where God would finally overthrow his enemies, was obvious; and 'harvest' is always a biblical picture of final judgement. No one else would share in the vindication (3,5). None came to the help of the Lord (Judg. 5:23), so he acted himself and alone but, even so, his power assured him of complete victory (5). No longer can God put action off. His Jubilee 'year of redemption' has come, and he must act (4). This 'treading of the winepress alone' (3) is in judgement upon others, not in silent suffering for others, as was that of Christ. Yet even Christ spoke sternly of coming judgement for those who had rejected his love (Matt. 23:33). The picture is still the same.

63:7–19 God's steadfast love

This, like many other passages in the Prophets, is almost a Psalm. It begins as a tranquil hymn of praise, meditating on Israel's past history, as in, say, Psalm 78. Then, in the last verses, it turns from this contemplation of God's past activity to prayer for his involvement in the needs of the present. This is a good theological pattern for us to follow today.

'Goodness and mercy', shown towards Israel, are the theme of the Psalm (7). Because God had acknowledged Israel as his people (8), he saved them from Egypt. The 'angel of his presence' went before them (Exod. 23:20) to lead them. He lifted and carried them like a father would carry a child (Deut. 1:31).

But the Psalm had sad notes as well. In spite of all God's loving care, Israel, even in those early days, had rebelled and grieved God (10). The Law of Moses is full of instances of this behaviour. Whenever this happened, God became like an enemy to them, and punished them, as indeed he was punishing them now. But then would come remembrance of the old days, the redemption under Moses (11). Once again Israel is reminded of God's marvellous deeds in leading his people through the Red Sea and out of Egypt (12,13). If God did that for them once, could he not do it again now? The simile of the horse galloping surefootedly over the desert, or the ox easily grazing its way down the hill to the valley, is one of the most beautiful pictures in the Old Testament (13,14). It represents the security of a people led by God, to whom God has given rest.

Then comes the cry of agony arising from the present. How can all these wonderful experiences of the past be related to Israel's present weakness and shame (15)? It seems as if God's love has departed from Israel (15). Indeed, it almost seems as though Abraham, and even their venerated ancestor Jacob – 'Israel' – have forgotten their descendants (16). If God is still their Father: why does he allow them to wander and remain hard-hearted (17)? Why does he allow their enemies to triumph over them (18), as though Israel were no longer his people (19)? So the Psalm ends with a great cry of despair which, in the next chapter, will pass into a prayer that God will manifest himself again in power.

TO THINK ABOUT: What is the value for us of other people's past experience of God, as recorded in the Bible? What is the value of our own past Christian experience? How can we relate this to our present needs? Does the feeling of desertion and abandonment come to all Christians at times? Does God really desert us? How should we cope with such feelings?

64 The wonder of God

This chapter begins with an appeal to God to come down in majesty and fire (1), as he had long ago on Mount Sinai where thunder and storm-cloud and flame made the Hebrews tremble (Exod. 19:16). But this, great though it is, is only God acting in nature. God's spiritual miracles are far more wonderful to those who trust him (4) and act with integrity. What God ever acted like this for his people? But there is another side to this, and we cannot have the one without the other. If God has this sort of moral nature, then our sin will rouse him to anger. We all appear as unclean to him, while our best attempts at self-justification are like disgusting filthy rags (6). How can we commend ourselves to a God as pure as this? No wonder that Israel felt as dead and impermanent as dry leaves, whirled away by the wind. There is no permanence apart from God, and no one looked for him (7). What was the use, if God had hidden his face from them and they had been abandoned to their sins?

There are, however, two great appeals still possible: God had called himself their Father (8) and, however sinful, they were still his children. God was also their creator (8). He had moulded man from clay, as a potter makes a vessel (Gen. 2:7). Jeremiah would boldly say that the Potter who made initially can also remake (Jer. 18:4). Here the thought is that creation in itself establishes a relationship that cannot be destroyed.

It is on the basis of this that Israel turns to God in anguish of spirit: how can all this be reconciled to the facts? Jerusalem and all the cities are in ruins, and even their beloved Temple, with its hallowed memories, is burnt to the ground (11). Everything that they loved has gone; how can God endure it? For the hardest thing of all for Israel to endure is not God's rebuke but God's silence.

TO THINK ABOUT: Why did God so often use physical manifestations of his presence in the Old Testament, and so rarely in the New Testament? Is there no value in the good things that people do? If not, what is the difference between 'being good' and 'being bad'? What are the different uses in the Bible of the 'potter and clay' metaphor? Why does God sometimes take from us the dearest things that we have?

65 God's reply

We might almost entitle this chapter, in all reverence, 'The anguish of God'. God has been accused of not listening to prayer, of not caring, of turning his face away. Instead, God says that he has always been pleading and welcoming (1). It was rebellious mankind who had ceaselessly rejected and rebuffed his love (12), love even to a people who deliberately chose to do all the things that grieved him (3). There follows a list of typical idolatrous practices of the time, forbidden in the Law of Moses. Even the loving patience of God has its limits, however: sooner or later God's forbearance will end, and his anger will blaze out (Rom. 2:4,5).

But, even in his anger, God will remember mercy: he will not totally destroy, but save a chosen remnant (8), and create of them a people to inherit his promises (9). So God's purposes will not fail. In spite of human sin and failure, his purposes will be seen by all to be accomplished. True, those who follow idols instead of the Lord will have no part in all this blessing: their anguish is that they refused to respond to the appeal of God while they had the opportunity (12). Their punishment is that they will see the blessedness of God's children, without entering into it themselves (13,14). How could they, when they have consistently and stubbornly refused the only way into it? God has, after all, only given them what they wanted; and now, too late, they have found that it does not and cannot satisfy.

But, for God's servants, there are ever greater and greater wonders to come. All the troubles and suffering of the past will be forgotten for ever (16). God will create everything anew – new heavens and a new earth (17) where there will be nothing but joy – God's rejoicing over his people and his people rejoicing in him. All the typical blessings of Old Testament days will be theirs – long life, prosperity, children. The curse will be no more: now at last the ideal kingdom of Isaiah 11 will come, with peace and harmony even in the animal world.

Note: verse 8 seems to refer to natural fermentation in the midst of a bunch of grapes while hanging over-long on the vine.

TO THINK ABOUT: Since Calvary, is it God who needs to be reconciled to man, or man who needs to be reconciled to God? Why does God endure sin for so long? Is it fair that, after death, there should be no 'second chance'? How are we in the New Testament age to understand these Old Testament blessings?

66 The end of the matter

The thought of rebuilding a ruined Temple and city had filled the minds of the Hebrews and, because it was important to them, they thought God would heed their prayer. But here he gently reminds them that in their enthusiasm for the Temple, they had lost sight of the God for whom they were building it (1). And yet, though God is so mighty, he sees and chooses the truly humble person (2), the very opposite of what one would assume. Those who choose their own ways, whether in open idolatry or in insincere lifeless ceremonial (for this may be the point of the contemptuous references to sacrifice, here compared to idolatry) will only bring suffering on themselves. But those who reverence God's word (5) have nothing to fear, even if they are rejected on earth.

The miraculous restoration of Zion is compared to a miraculous birth, a birth which takes place before any labour-pangs have been felt (7). Just so God will restore Israel: she will not toil to accomplish it, for it will all be God's work. And how can Israel be sure that God will do all this? Because God has already begun to work, and that is the guarantee that he will finish the task (9). Centuries later, Paul was to say that the God who has begun a good work in the life of the Christian will continue and complete it right up until the last great day (Phil. 1:6). God's restoration of Zion is, however, only the beginning of his work. Through her, he will also bring blessing to others (11). Jerusalem is seen as a nursing mother, with milk enough for all her children: all will share her richness.

The book ends on a strong eschatological note, describing every aspect of the Last Days. God will reveal himself, as we have seen, to his servants; his enemies will only know his anger (14). 'Chariots of fire' is an Old Testament description of God in his majesty (2 Kings 2:11). The nations will be gathered from the world's end (18) to worship the Lord, and even they may hold the honoured positions of priests and Levites in God's 'brave new world' (21). Now, at last, all mankind will acknowledge God; but even so there will be the solemn reminder of those who chose rebellion rather than submission to God.

TO THINK ABOUT: If the whole universe is too small to contain God (1 Kings 8:27), why did he command Israel to build him a Temple? Why have we no temple in the new covenant? What is God's purpose in calling out the church from all humanity? Will all nations one day be saved? Why did Jesus quote the rather terrifying last verse of Isaiah (Mark 9:48)?

Jeremiah: Introduction

The book of Jeremiah is not hard to understand, but it is a complicated book because Jeremiah 'tells it as it is', never hiding from us his own inmost feelings – even, at times, his feelings of rebellion against God. That is what makes the book so valuable to us spiritually. Perhaps that also accounts for its disjointedness and apparent lack of order, for Jeremiah was not interested in developing a long and logical argument, or in sustaining some careful scheme. Besides, his prophecies were initially *spoken*: they were apparently not written down till God's command in 36:2. Perhaps this 'scroll' represents the earlier part of our book of Jeremiah, or most of it; for it will be remembered that when King Jehoiakim burnt the scroll, Jeremiah not only re-wrote it, but added many similar prophecies to it (36:32). So (as in the case of any Israelite prophet) we have, first, an account of Jeremiah's call in chapter 1, followed by prophecies both of judgement and of mercy, until approximately chapter 36, the presumed end of the scroll.

Chapters 37 to 45 are mostly historical chapters in prose (prophecy was usually written in verse), giving the historical background of the period. Chapters 46 to 51 seem to be a collection of Jeremiah's prophecies against foreign nations, not Israel; and chapter 52 is a final historical appendix in prose, linking us again with the book of Kings (2 Kings 24:18–25:30). We must not therefore look for an orderly historical sequence in the book: neither Jeremiah nor his editor (was it his friend Baruch the scribe, of chapter 45?) was interested in that. Jeremiah's sole interest was in God's message to Judah, whether judgement (as usually) or mercy (as in the so-called 'Book of Comfort', chapters 30 to 31). At the very heart of the book stands God's promise to his people of a 'New Covenant' (31:31–33). This revelation is perhaps Jeremiah's greatest contribution to the Old Testament for, although all his work can be dated between the death of Josiah (the last King of Judah to worship God) and the extinction of the tiny state of Judah in 586 BC or the years immediately following, Jeremiah looked far beyond the disaster to God's triumph in the future.

Jeremiah: Contents

1 Jeremiah's visions

This chapter is the keynote of the whole book of Jeremiah, for it contains the account of his call by God to be a prophet. It was not a call that could be refused, for it rested on a prior choice by God of Jeremiah before his birth. In fact, the whole purpose of his creation is only to be found in God's purpose that Jeremiah should be a 'prophet to the (non-Israelite) nations' (5). When Jeremiah demurs, as most biblical prophets do, in his case on the grounds of youth and inexperience, God encourages him (7,8) and tells him of the greatness of the task already prepared for him.

But God not only gives Jeremiah his word of promise; he also gives signs, to make his word doubly sure. Since Jeremiah is a prophet (the old name was a 'see-er') it was only right that he should have some supporting visions. However, the visions of Jeremiah are very different from, let us say, the visions of Ezekiel: they are much more like the common experience of thoughtful Christians today. He sees an ordinary natural object, then God makes that natural object a symbol and conveyor of spiritual truth. Jeremiah's visions are therefore much closer to the parables of Christ than to the visions found in apocalyptic books.

He sees, for instance, a branch of almond, the 'watchful' or 'wide-awake' tree, as its Hebrew name means – because its blossoms are the first to wake after the cold winter, before there are even leaves on the trees. He is reminded by God, through this, of God's watchfulness over his promises (12). And he sees a cooking pot, precariously balanced on an open fire, slowly tipping its boiling contents from the north side (the Hebrews were more conscious of compass directions than we are today). Through this, God tells Jeremiah that judgement from the north is about to boil over Israel, a judgement for their idolatry (16) and faithlessness to God. This is no message of ease and comfort.

In the light of these visions and these promises of God, Jeremiah is called to be like a besieged city himself, as Jerusalem will be. He is called to live a life of perpetual opposition with no praise or success, but only with the assurance that because God is with him there will be no defeat, and God's purpose will be accomplished.

TO THINK ABOUT: Should we ask for 'signs' that God has called us? If not, why not? If so, what sort of signs? How should a Christian judge 'success' and 'failure'?

2:1–13 The desert honeymoon

Again and again, in revulsion against the cold-heartedness and religious faithlessness of their own day, the minds of the prophets go back wistfully to Israel's earliest experience of salvation, as a Christian might remember wistfully his or her conversion days. Israel is pictured as following the Lord into the desert, for love of him. To him she was like the sacred first-fruits of a harvest, dedicated to God. No farmer would dare eat these first-fruits, lest retribution followed. So none dared to harm God's people. How had God ever failed them, that they should desert him (5)? They had forgotten the threefold miracle – the redemption from Egypt, the leading through the hostile desert, and the bringing into the fertile land of Canaan (6,7). It is no accident that the keynote of a book like Deuteronomy is 'remember!' (Deut. 5:15), nor that, in the New Testament, the Lord told his disciples, 'Do this in remembrance of me' (1 Cor. 11:24). To forget God's gracious acts to us is to risk Israel's fate. They defiled Canaan, the land he promised them, as soon as they entered it, by behaving exactly like the heathen Canaanites whom they had dispossessed. Priests, scribes, rulers, prophets – all alike became faithless to God: all those who were in positions of special authority and who should therefore have given a good example to Israel (8).

Does Israel not realise what an awful thing she has done, in abandoning the God who saved her from Egypt in order to follow Baal? No other nation in the whole of the world, from the furthest islands of the Mediterranean to the desert dwellers of the East, has ever done such a thing. Idolaters they might be, but at least they have clung to their ancestral gods: only Israel has abandoned hers (11). Jeremiah shows not only the ingratitude of Israel but also her folly. She has left the flowing fresh waters of a spring, and instead hewed out for herself cisterns that only hold flat-tasting rainwater, and even then cannot contain it for the water continually leaks away through the cracks in the rock. No better description could be given of a people who have left the living God to seek, always in vain, their own self-satisfaction in things of this world.

TO THINK ABOUT: In what ways is our Christian experience today sometimes like that of Israel's in the Old Testament? Why does the coming of the Holy Spirit not make it totally different? Why is 're-membering' so important? Why is it that this world can never satisfy us?

2:14 –37 Israel's sin

In the book of Jeremiah, 'Israel' is used loosely for the whole of God's people (14). When, however, 'Israel' is used in contrast with 'Judah' (3:10) it refers only to the northern kingdom, already in exile. So the question is: why are God's people suffering as they are (14)? The country is ravaged by Babylon from the north and Egypt has invaded the south. Playing off one 'great power' against another is of no avail (18) for the true cause of her suffering is not political but is because she has left her God (19). There follows a vivid account of Israel's wilful behaviour, for it is not by accident that she has left God but by deliberate, reiterated choice: is not the same true of all rejection of God? She is like a draught-animal or plough-ox that has run away; she is like a cultivated vine gone wild; she is like a garment stained so badly that no known detergent can clean it. She is as shameless in her pursuit of Baal as a bitch in heat (in our city culture we must substitute dogs for camels). This is strong language, if not coarse language. That the gentle Jeremiah could use it shows how strongly he felt about Israel's sin. If the covenant that God has made with Israel was as close as a marriage bond, then to worship Baal was as disgusting as adultery, and the prophets deliberately used language that shocks, so that Israel might be jolted into realising the enormity of her sin. Some modern evangelists use similar 'shock tactics' today.

But the day of reckoning always comes (26). When disaster is impending, Israel's gods of wood and stone (26,27) cannot save her; and then she has the affrontery to plead with God to save her. Fickle as she is, bloodstained as her hands are, she thinks so lightly of sin that she is confident that God has already forgiven her (35). How can he? The same shallowness shows in Israel's foreign policy. At one time she had turned to Assyria for help; now she turns to Egypt, but it will do her just as little good. If God has already rejected the nations that are Israel's mainstay and support, what use will it be to rely upon them? There is no escape there from God's coming judgement.

Note: verse 34. It was legitimate to shed the blood of a thief as he broke into a house in the night, for the householders might not know whether the thief was armed or not. Otherwise, to shed 'innocent blood' brought God's vengeance.

TO THINK ABOUT: Why was Israel so slow to admit that the disasters were her own fault? Why was it so easy for Israel to 'revert to type'? Can a reborn Christian do this too?

3:1–18 Can Israel return?

Is Jeremiah's mission pointless? Is there any hope that, if Judah returned, God would receive her back again to himself? The Law of Moses said clearly that a wife, once divorced and remarried, might not return to her first husband, even if he were willing to take her back (Deut. 24:1–4). Israel has not just been casually unfaithful to God: she has been deliberately and consistently unfaithful in worshipping countless foreign gods. She has not just been an unfaithful wife; she has been like a shameless prostitute (1,2). Even God's punishment (seen in the withholding of the usual yearly rains (3)) had not brought Judah back to God in penitence. Her sin was worse than that of Israel, her 'sister', for Judah had seen what God had already done to Israel, a century and a half before, and yet she had not learned the lesson (8). Any repentance was sham, not real (10), for it did not affect Judah's life. Compared with Judah, even disloyal Israel was less guilty: even she would therefore have the opportunity to return to God (12). All that she needs to do is to acknowledge her guilt.

In verses 14 to 18, God can restrain himself no longer. He pours out his heart in appeal to his sinful people to turn again to him, appealing to the nation now as his children rather than as his bride. As usual, with his call come promises: he will gather them back to Zion, even if only a small remnant (14). Had they been led astray by false leaders? He will give them good shepherds like David, men 'after God's own heart' (15). They will not even miss the lost Ark, burnt with the Temple in the Babylonian conquest of 586 BC, for Jerusalem herself, not just the Ark of the covenant, will be Yahweh's throne (17). Two results will follow: 'evangelisation' of the heathen nations, who will flock to Jerusalem to worship Yahweh; and unity among brethren, for once again North and South will unite into one kingdom, as in the days of David and Solomon.

TO THINK ABOUT: In what ways does God's love go beyond the demands of the Law of Moses? Does Hosea help us to understand the love of God? Does Christ, in the New Testament, say anything that helps us to understand this? Why does repentance always involve acknowledgment of sin? Within Christianity, have evangelism and the unity of believers any connection with repentance?

3:19–4:4 God's terms

Jeremiah slips back again here into poetry, as God describes poignantly what his plans for Israel had been and how they were frustrated by Israel's treachery to him (19,20). But now there comes a wonderful response to the appeal of God: Israel, in tears, is heard seeking a reconciliation (21). At last her people have found out that the worship of Baal can never satisfy (23,24). At last they are prepared to admit their sins before God (25). This is good and necessary; but repentance goes a great deal further than that. Both idolatry (4:1) and injustice (4:2) must be firmly and deliberately put aside: repentance involves both religion and ethics. To take an oath 'As Yahweh lives' (2) is not merely to correct the misuse of Yahweh's name (as in Exod. 20:7); it is something far more fundamental. In the ancient world, men swore by the most stable fact that they knew. If the fact that 'Yahweh lives' is the most sure thing in the world to us, then God is at the very centre of our lives. Seeing such a dramatic change in our outlook will win others for God (2). The root of evangelism lies in deep personal repentance and change of heart. That is what Jeremiah means when he tells them to break up the hard fallow ground of their old lives, lest the gospel be sown only on top of the thorns of their old lives. It is not enough to bear the outward sign of the old covenant – circumcision – on their bodies; their hearts must be marked by the change.

'Uncircumcised in heart' denotes one who may bear all the outward marks of religion, but with no corresponding inner reality. That has always been the tragedy of Israel in the past, and a shallow repentance would leave it unchanged. Is it to be no different in the future? This in turn is why Jeremiah (31:33) stresses the essential inwardness and reality of the 'new covenant' that God will make with his people in later days.

TO THINK ABOUT: Can we really frustrate God's plans for us, or only delay them? What did John the Baptist say about repentance? What about the seed sown among the thorns in the Parable of the Sower? In the new covenant, even after the gift of the Spirit, is there still a danger of hypocrisy? If so, why?

4:5–31 The invaders

In this vivid poem the onset of the dreaded armies from the north is described. The north is always the ominous quarter for Israel: to the south lay Egypt, and to the east all her sister-nations like Aram, Ammon, Moab and Edom. But the north was the unknown and invaders had been bursting out from there since the days of Abraham and Genesis 14. Sumer, Assyria, Babylonia, Persia: in turn they poured down in their hordes and in each case it was seen as the judgement of God. At this stage of Judah's history Babylon will be the invader, but the picture only clarifies gradually. At first it is the boiling pot, spilling over from the north (1:14). Here, it is still only a vague menace from the north. Before the book is through Jeremiah will speak openly of the king of Babylon. Israel must recognise God's hand in judgement in the events of world history; do we?

Their first reaction is terror; the second is to feel that they have been deceived, presumably by the words of the false prophets who had consistently told them that all was well when it was not (10). Now the scorching 'hamsin', the hot blast from the desert, is withering everything. The enemy arrives yet nearer and nearer: Dan, Ephraim, Judah, Jerusalem (15,16). Jerusalem has brought all this on herself in turning away from God (18); but even so, it is still not too late to repent and be saved (14). Jeremiah himself is plunged into anguish when he sees prophetically the whole country ravaged (19,20). Even God marvels that his children could be so stupid: they cannot see either that *he* is bringing this disaster on them, or his *purpose* in doing so.

Then, as often in the prophets, a picture of temporal judgement passes into one of eternal judgement: the scene shifts to the 'last days', to a reversal of the process of creation as told in Genesis. The uninhabited earth reverts to chaos again; not even the birds remain in a land where there is no sign of life (23–25). In the midst, Zion, like a rejected prostitute, cries in vain for help from her enemies.

TO THINK ABOUT: Does God still work out his judgements in history? If so, how, and with what purpose? Why, in the Bible, is it the sign of the false prophet that he says 'All is well'? What are the biblical definitions of wisdom and folly? Does the Bible teach that this world will revert to chaos at the end? Could atomic war play a part in this?

5:1–19 Jerusalem or Sodom?

God would have spared even Sodom, in the days of Abraham, if he had found in her as many as ten righteous men (Gen. 18:32). But how can he spare Jerusalem when he cannot even find in her *one* righteous man (1)? What God demands is justice and integrity to show the reality of Judah's faith in him; and he can find no one to satisfy these requirements. Their great oath is 'As truly as Yahweh lives', which sounds orthodox enough; but if they really believed that he was 'the living God' they could not act like this (2). They will not take note of God's punishment, designed to bring them to repentance (Heb. 12:11). Jeremiah is at his wits' end. At first he thinks that they are so blind because they are uneducated and have no knowledge of God's law (4); but then he finds that the literate groups are just the same. Opposition to God and his will is not determined by our class in society, but is part of society itself, for it is part of our perverse and foolish human nature. If the people of Jerusalem have themselves closed the only door to salvation that God has provided, the door of repentance, then disaster is certain (6).

God speaks in anguish: how can he, a God of justice, pardon those who have abused all his gifts only to sin more and more (7–9)? Baal is more real to them than Yahweh; they even swear by Baal's name (7). So the pruner's merciless knife must shear through the vineyard. These are dead branches, for Judah and Israel have been faithless to God. Their prophets have lied to them in saying that disaster would not come from God (12); they have become mere empty windbags, instead of being spirit-filled (13). By contrast, Jeremiah, the true prophet, will speak words of fire that will set the bush ablaze with judgement. For God is bringing the ancient nation of Babylon, in all her military might, to conquer Israel. Even here, because of God's love, a tiny remnant will be left ('I will not destroy you completely', 10,18). The old 'tit for tat' of the Law of Moses (Exod. 21:24) is fulfilled: if Israel has served foreign gods in Israel, she must now serve foreigners in a distant land.

TO THINK ABOUT: Does God still demand justice and integrity from his people today? What does that involve for us? Would God see our society today as being like that of Sodom? Does he still bring judgement on corrupt societies? Why does knowledge about God not necessarily make people better? Why is there hope in the 'remnant' concept?

Judah in Jeremiah's day is like Judah in Christ's day: they have no spiritual perception (21). The Lord expressed the same thought when talking about his parables (Mark 4:12). Can it be that they have forgotten the power of God the creator (22)? Is that why they despise his warnings? Or is it that they have forgotten the goodness of God the creator in giving them harvest and fruitfulness (24)? Certainly they have forgotten God. They show it by 'catching men', but not in the sense commanded by Christ to his apostles (Luke 5:10): they have become rich and powerful by injustice and rapacity. They do not defend the helpless, the orphans, the poor (28). On people such as these God's judgement always comes. Often, as in the days of Jeremiah, it comes in what we see as the natural processes of history, but which is ultimately the work of God's hand (29).

How can this terrible moral blindness persist? Because the prophets are lying, the priests listen to the prophets, and the people are happy with the whole arrangement (31). Of course they are; this sort of 'gospel' (like Baal-worship) is very congenial to natural man, since it has no stumbling-block in it. But all this tissue of deceits will be useless when the disaster falls and Benjamin, Tekoa, and Beth-haccerem are all suddenly engulfed by the invading army from the north (6:1). Now the tide rolls right to the walls of Jerusalem, and the attack will come at any moment (4,5). The trees are cut to make battering rams; earth is piled for siege mounds outside the city (6). The disaster cannot be withheld any longer (11) and, when it comes, all will be involved in it; God's judgement is universal. It is bad enough that prophet and priest alike are dishonest (13); worse still that they say 'All is well' when nothing is well. For such men, as for those whom they mislead, there is no hope; but their condemnation is the greater.

TO THINK ABOUT: Why, in the Old Testament, are wisdom and folly seen more in moral than in intellectual terms? What can we know about God from his work in creating and sustaining the world? Can this knowledge alone lead us to salvation? Should we still protect the poor and helpless? Why? What relation has this to salvation?

6:16–30 God the refiner

We tend to think that what is new must therefore be good and right:
but sometimes it is the old that is right, and so it was with Israel. God
recalls them to the 'old paths' (16), to the Law that they have rejected
(19). That, for Israel, was the good road, the only road that led to rest
(16). In the New Testament, Christ said the same about those who
came to him and took up his yoke (Matt. 11:28,29). But God's people
stubbornly refused to hear God's voice; so disaster must come, the
bitter fruit of what they have sown (19). They honestly thought that
Yahweh cared about their expensive imported incense and sugar cane
(20), the costly gifts they gave him; but their sacrifices were an anath-
ema to him. This was the continual message of the Old Testament
prophets, which incredulous Israel could never really believe. No wonder that God would 'put' stumbling-blocks in their way (21): it was his
very nature that proved a stumbling-block to them.

Again we switch to a vivid description of the invading hordes of
cavalry from the north, and the consequent terror of the inhabitants.
Some have seen it as referring to raids by wild Scythian tribesmen
from the north, but it seems better to see it as a prophetic picture of
the Babylonians and their mercenary troops.

Then the scene shifts, and we see the reason for such a terrible
invasion: God is refining his people in the fire of affliction. Jeremiah
is like the expectant silversmith, standing by to report the success of
the operation (27). But there is no success. The fire is there, the bellows
blow, the smelter works, yet the dross remains, and no pure silver
results (29). The silversmith can only describe the whole crucible as
worthless, and reject it. This is how Yahweh has found Israel to be.
All her affliction has only confirmed her in her wrong attitudes instead
of changing them.

**TO THINK ABOUT: How can we, as Christians, both hold fast to the
old, and yet adapt to the new? Does God not enjoy beautiful music
and beautiful services? What are the various reasons for affliction in
our lives? What different reactions can it produce in us? Why does it
not automatically produce good results in a Christian?**

7:1–29 A Temple doomed

When Christ spoke his stern words about the coming doom on the Temple at Jerusalem (Matt. 24:2) all who heard him would have remembered this passage. For Jeremiah was standing at the gate of Solomon's Temple, one of the wonders of the ancient world. It was the place chosen by God for his dwelling among men (1 Kings 6:13), as the Israelites claimed. They were not wrong to flock through the gates for worship (2): it was indeed Yahweh's Temple, as they proudly reiterated (4). But they were utterly wrong to think that they could live as sinfully as they pleased, break all the Ten Commandments, worship other gods, and still be accepted when they came to the Temple in worship (10). They had made the Temple a robbers' hideout; did they really think they were safe there when judgement struck?

There was one thing that they had forgotten. Long before the Temple had been built, God had made his earthly home at little Shiloh, in the hills of Ephraim (12). Yet, because of the sins of Eli's house, the Ark had been captured, Shiloh left in ruins, and the house of Eli left under a curse (1 Sam. 3). Even the whole northern kingdom ('Ephraim') had now gone into exile. What God had done to Shiloh, God would do to Jerusalem, for he is no respecter of persons. Judah now must go into exile herself (15). Worse still, Jeremiah was forbidden to intercede for his people, as Abraham at the last had been prevented from interceding any further for Sodom (Gen. 18:33). Intercession was of no use: the whole family (men, women, and children) are all united in idolatrous worship, even in the heart of holy Jerusalem itself (18). They may as well eat all the sacrifices themselves, instead of giving them to God. The heart of the Law given to their forefathers had been to demand obedience, not sacrifice (23). But Israel had consistently refused to listen, from the days of the exodus onwards (24). Prophet after prophet had spoken in vain; now Jeremiah must speak in vain too (27).

7:30–8:12 A world out of joint

If relationships with God are distorted, everything else becomes distorted too. Idols in God's Temple will lead to a 'Tophet' (a 'burning-place') in the Valley of Hinnom's son, where Judah offer up their firstborn babies as burnt sacrifices. This was the ultimate blasphemy: they honestly thought these were offerings to God, but God says in anguish that such an idea had never entered his mind (31). The punishment will be that, in the doom of Jerusalem, the pleasant Valley of Hinnom (the short form of the name) will be called 'Slaughter Valley', so full will it be with corpses from the siege. Indeed, in later days 'Gehenna' became a synonym for Hell, the rubbish dump and paupers' graveyard of Jerusalem, with fires ever burning and worms ever active. That is what sin can do to any Eden. They had defiled the valley by their awful acts – now all would see the results.

The kings of Judah had worshipped, not the true God, but sun, moon and stars, and now their sepulchres will be looted and rifled during the siege of Jerusalem, and their bones will be scattered on the ground before the sun and moon, which they had served (8:2). To remain unburied was the ultimate horror and disgrace of the ancient world. Why was this fate to be theirs? Because, says the prophet, they cling to illusions (5). Even migratory birds have wisdom and understand God's natural laws (7) but God's people seem blind and impervious. This distortion goes further: the scribes boast of their possession of God's word (8) and, since the rediscovery of the Law Book in the Temple, this was true in a sense. But the man of warped mind will misunderstand and distort even God's word, with the result that he will reject God's plan. Such wisdom is of no use to them.

Note: In 621 BC, the Law Book was rediscovered in the Temple where it had presumably been hidden in the oppressive days of Manasseh (2 Kings 22:8). This sparked off reforms in Judah.

TO THINK ABOUT: Why is it that, if our thinking about God becomes warped, our thinking about other matters is equally affected? Is it possible to quote the Bible and yet be thoroughly unbiblical? How can we avoid this?

8:13–9:26 The prophet's complaint

Jeremiah is utterly overwhelmed. It is God's will to overthrow his own people: and they richly deserve it (13), for they are like a fruit tree without fruit. In the wilderness, God had sweetened bitter water for Israel (Exod. 15:25) and healed their snake bites (Num. 21:9); but not now (14,17). Too late, they realise the reason: Zion's King has left her (19). That was what happened at Shiloh, when a dying woman had named her son Ichabod ('where is Israel's glory?' 1 Sam. 4:21).

But Jeremiah is no passive onlooker. He shares in the agony of his people (21) as Paul was to do later (Rom. 9). If he could, he would pitch his tent in the desert away from his people (9:2), just as the tabernacle, with Moses and Joshua, had been obliged to move away from the camp of Israel because of Israel's sin (Exod. 33:7). Judah was lying and false through and through: they were all 'Jacobs' (supplanters, deceivers) who had never been changed by grace into 'Israels' (4). They might say 'Peace!' as a greeting to their neighbour, but all the time they were secretly plotting their neighbour's ruin (8). God's judgement must come for this: Jerusalem will be a pile of ruins, and Judah's farmland will go back to bush again (10).

Jeremiah would one day be on trial for his life because of these inflammatory words; but they were nevertheless God's words (11). And the reason for the judgement? The people have forsaken God's law, and followed the Baals, just like their ancestors had done (14). So God will scatter them among the nations (16) and the world dispersion of the Jews will begin. Half in bitter mockery, half in despair, Jeremiah parodies the sort of lament raised by the professional mourning-women of the day (17–21), who also appear in the New Testament (Mark 5:38).

So what is the end of the whole matter? Man must not boast in his wisdom, strength, or wealth; only in the knowledge of Yahweh and of his nature. Otherwise, Judah becomes no different from the heathen nations around her (25,26).

TO THINK ABOUT: Why does God lay so much stress on spiritual fruits, if we are not actually saved by what we do? Why did both Jeremiah and Paul feel such concern for their people? In what ways should we be similarly concerned? Why does the New Testament say that we, in our turn, should only boast in the cross? What does 'uncircumcised in heart' mean? What would correspond to it today?

10:1–25 Contrast: Yahweh and idols

Mockery of idols was a constant and necessary theme in the days of the prophets, when idolatry and magic (with accompanying immorality) were the great dangers for Israel. So Jeremiah begins by showing how absurd it is to worship something made by humans (3), as absurd as the modern worship of science and technology. He compares idols to mere scarecrows: they can do neither good nor harm (5). But Israel's 'Living God' (10) is totally different – he rules the world (7). Not only so, but he is also the great creator (12) and still controls his universe. Earthquake (10), thunder, rainstorm, lightning, hurricane (13) – all these are symbols of his power. Not only are the idols shamed by this, so are the idol-makers (14).

But they are more than ashamed. Now that they have realised the terrible truth, they are in a panic (17). Mass evacuation of Jerusalem follows on the realisation of God's imminent judgement. Metaphors of disaster tumble over one another in quick succession: a besieged city, a mortally wounded man, a collapsed tent, a bereaved family, a scattered flock (17–21). Already, in prophetic imagination, Jeremiah actually hears the distant roar of the army from the north that will reduce Judah's towns to bush land again (22).

Even in this extremity, he turns to God in prayer. He pleads with Yahweh because of the very helplessness of man. If Yahweh punishes too severely, Judah will be annihilated, and the whole purpose of the discipline will be lost (24). So Abraham had pleaded for Sodom, on the grounds of God's justice (Gen. 18:25). So Moses had pleaded for sinning Israel, on the grounds of God's promise (Exod. 32:13). Jeremiah asks the very human question: why cannot God vent his wrath on the heathen, instead of on Israel, his own people? But even while he asks the question, he knows the answer only too well, and the next chapter makes it plain.

TO THINK ABOUT: What are the great idols of our civilisation today? How can we, as Christians, show their emptiness to others? Can we still believe that God controls winds, storms etc, now that we understand their physical causes? What is God's purpose in punishing his people? Could we today pray Jeremiah's prayer about the heathen?

11:1–23 The broken covenant

Jeremiah began his ministry in the reign of King Josiah (1:2). It was in Josiah's reign that the book of Deuteronomy was re-discovered, during the repairs to the Temple which had been left in dilapidation during the reign of the reactionary King Manasseh. So Jeremiah often reflects both the thought and the language of Deuteronomy, and this is one such place. Jeremiah must have heartily approved of Josiah's reforms, which were based on Deuteronomy. Whether, however, he actually went crusading about the country to preach Deuteronomy, as is sometimes suggested on the basis of this passage, is quite uncertain. Here he talks of the old covenant. Just as Deuteronomy told of God's blessing for those who kept the covenant, so it told of God's curse for those who broke it (Deut. 27:15–28:68). Just as in Deuteronomy the people were commanded to set their 'Amen' to this blessing and cursing, to show their agreement, so Jeremiah does now (5). All that was demanded of Israel in response was obedience. Then God would be their God, and they would be his people. This was the heart of the covenant message, and this was what Jeremiah was to proclaim (6).

But this was the one thing which Israel had never done, ever since the days of Egypt, in spite of all God's warnings to them (7). So now God is bringing down upon them all the curses of the covenant; curses which they cannot escape (11). Worse still, even if they cry to God then, he will not hear them. Like Esau, they are past the point of no return (Heb. 12:17). True, they may pray then to all their idols, but will find out too late that their idols cannot help them and that the Lord will not help them. Jeremiah is not even permitted to pray for them (14): God forbids intercession for unrepentant Judah. But Judah's guilt becomes even clearer. Jeremiah finds that even his own relatives in the priestly village of Anathoth are plotting to murder him, to silence his voice. Jeremiah was like a lamb being led to the abattoir, until God revealed that danger to him. Small wonder that God will bring doom even on little Anathoth.

TO THINK ABOUT: What do 'blessing' and 'curse' mean in the Bible? Are they just the inevitable spiritual results of our actions? Why would God not hear the prayers of Judah? Why was Jeremiah forbidden to pray for them? In what ways was Jeremiah like Christ? Could a Christian pray for God's vengeance on his enemies, as Jeremiah did (20)?

12:1–17 Jeremiah's puzzle

One of the refreshing things about the book of Jeremiah is that (like Job and some of the Psalms) we can see right into the writer's heart, and understand some of his deepest feelings. He never pretends to understand all God's dealings with him, or that there are easy solutions to all of life's problems. Here, it is the old question: why do these people, whose views are so warped and whose lives are so twisted, succeed so well in this life (1)? They are always talking about God, but it is sheer hypocrisy (2). Jeremiah thinks that surely they, not he, should be the sheep dragged to the abattoirs (3).

God does not deal with this by rebuke. He does not even deal with it by answering the question. Instead, he simply warns Jeremiah that even greater testings lie ahead: if he stumbles over God's way of working in such a simple thing, how will he cope with the far greater tests to faith that will follow when Jerusalem falls (5)? That was the sort of robust comfort that Christ gave to John the Baptist when he was in prison and his faith wavered (Matt. 11:4–6). It was robust comfort, but it worked, both in the case of John and of Jeremiah. Both of them stood firm to the last.

True, God says, he has abandoned his heritage to the enemy: this is the anger of God (13). Like the man in the New Testament (Matt. 13:27), Judah will sow wheat, but only reap thorns (13). Yet the time will come when God will rescue Judah (14) and treat the other nations as they treated her, bringing them into exile, too. But if this is to be the 'tit for tat' of the Law of Moses (Lev. 24:20), it must go the whole way. God's people will come home after exile, and so will these Gentile enemies, if only they turn to God (16). Jew and Gentile will be one at last, in the knowledge of God; the Old Testament can rise no higher. This is truly a triumphant faith.

TO THINK ABOUT: Was Jeremiah wrong in asking God to punish the wicked? Why was it necessary in those days for him to make such a request? Would it be right for us today to ask it? What is the deepest answer to Jeremiah's problem? When were Jew and Gentile truly made one?

13 The spoilt loincloth

Scholars are divided as to whether what is described here was an actual incident or a prophetic vision of the prophet; and as to whether the Euphrates mentioned was the famous river of that name, or a smaller stream much closer to Jerusalem, also known. As far as prophetic symbolism is concerned, it would be heightened if this were the Euphrates that ran through Babylon, and if this was an actual event. Both of these are the positions taken here. The loincloth (corresponding to our modern 'briefs') was the piece of clothing that clung to the body; so Israel and Judah were intended to cling to God. But God would nevertheless put them away, as Jeremiah put his loincloth away (4). God would bury his people in obscurity in Babylon, as Jeremiah had buried his loincloth in a hole by the bank of the Euphrates. Presumably, a new loincloth, never yet washed, would be more likely to show damp and mould marks than one previously washed: or the thought may simply be the ruin of a garment that had been almost brand new. The point is that what had been valuable is now utterly valueless. The thought seems to be that the exile and its experience of suffering, while it might lead to humbling and return for some, would end in destruction for others who persisted in their pride. Jeremiah is famous for his vivid imagery and symbolism but none brings a more clear or chilling meaning than this: for some, God's judgement is not corrective but final.

Similarly, he seizes on the simile of the clay wine jugs. The reeling of a drunken man is often compared in the Bible to people reeling under blows (as we speak of a boxer being 'punch-drunk'). God's judgement will come on all in Jerusalem, from highest to lowest (13) and, as the empty clay wine jars or wine jugs were smashed by the careless drinkers, so will they be (14). Lest there should be any doubt as to who was intended, the king and the queen-mother are directly addressed (18) and warned of the coming deportation. But it was a fate richly deserved by Jerusalem (22); she cannot change her nature (23), any more than a man can change the colour of his skin.

TO THINK ABOUT: Why did the deportation not achieve its purpose for some of the exiles? What qualities in us can prevent God's work? If Jerusalem could not change her nature, why was she to blame?

14 Drought and famine

It is important to remember that Judah depended on annual rains for existence, and that good rains were always seen as God's blessing and a proof of his favour, while drought was seen as God's direct punishment for sin. In Israel, therefore, drought was usually a time of fasting and prayer and repentance, in hope that God would relent and send rain. Nowadays, in Christian times, we would not associate these things so directly, nor see God's blessing so obviously in merely outward occurrences.

This passage begins with a vivid picture of total drought: even the wild animals of the semi-desert, accustomed to arid conditions, are dying (5,6). So, naturally, Jeremiah confesses the sin of his people (7) and begs for forgiveness (9). To his horror, God forbids him to pray for Judah (11), as he had forbidden Samuel to pray for Saul (1 Sam. 15:11; 16:1). This is the biblical way of saying that God has determined on a particular course of action, and that nothing will turn him aside from it (12). Again, the horrified Jeremiah quotes to God the so-called 'prophets of salvation' (13) – those who assure Judah of peace, not wars and famine (13). But God says sadly that he had never sent such prophets (14). Since they prophesy lies in God's name, they too must share in the judgement of their people (15). It is this knowledge that earns for Jeremiah the title of 'the weeping prophet'. As the Lord wept over the coming destruction of Jerusalem, so did Jeremiah, long before (17). All that he can do now is to appeal to God to remember his covenant with his people (21) and to re-assert Israel's faith that only the God of Israel can send the needed rain (22); the pagan idols cannot send it. This was the faith that had held Elijah firm at Mount Carmel (1 Kings 18, which should be read in detail as comparison). It was indeed the knowledge that only God could give rain which made his deliberate withholding of rain so agonising, and created the problem for Jeremiah.

TO THINK ABOUT: Should we today see drought as God's punishment for our sins? If not, do so-called 'natural disasters' like drought have any spiritual significance? Does the New Testament ever tell us to stop praying for anyone? Does God 'change his mind' in answer to our prayers? If not, why do we pray?

15:1–9 No more intercession!

We have seen in 14:11 that God forbade Jeremiah to pray for the people. Even if they fasted and prayed themselves, God would not listen (14:12). Here the message is reiterated even more grimly: even if Moses and Samuel, those mighty intercessors for Israel, were to pray for them, God would still not be turned aside from his purpose of punishment (1). As in 14:12, sword, famine, and pestilence are to be their doom; but these are also the group whom God has destined for captivity (2), and here we may see a ray of hope, for some of the last group would return. For the first time, while not exculpating the Judaeans of his own day, Jeremiah lays the blame squarely on King Manasseh's shoulders since (2 Kings 21:11) he had 'made Judah to sin', as Jeroboam had made Israel to sin (1 Kings 14:16). It is not God who has rejected Judah, but Judah who has rejected God (6).

At last God's patience is exhausted. He will scatter them like a farmer threshing wheat, who uses a hayfork to toss the sheaves in the air (7). But even here there is a hope of mercy: the farmer winnows his wheat so that he may lose the chaff and stalks, but keep the grain. But, at the moment, the thought is not of mercy but the totality of the destruction. Judah will be a land full of widows and bereaved mothers (8). To those of us who remember a world war, this has the grim touch of reality: an army will march out, and never return. The 'mother of seven sons' is a Hebrew picture of complete happiness and confidence; now, at one blow, all are gone (9). Even the remnant, the tiny group taken prisoner, will endure all the rigours of a prisoner-of-war camp.

TO THINK ABOUT: What made Moses and Samuel such mighty intercessors for Israel? Was it something in their own experience? Was it fair to blame Manasseh for Judah's apostasy? Why is it dangerous to hold a leading position? Why did God not continue to put up with Judah's sin? Would it have done Judah any good if he had? Is God's punishment vindictive or corrective, or does it have another purpose?

15:10–21 Jeremiah's outburst

We have seen that one of the human points about Jeremiah is that he never hides his fears and doubts from God, and so we see him in all his weakness as well as his strength. Here, as in chapter 20, he comes within an ace of giving up the struggle altogether. He wishes that he had never been born – as Job did (Job 3:3, but read the whole chapter). Jeremiah was by nature a man of peace: but God had called him to deliver a message which made him as hated as the notorious Eastern moneylenders (10). To make it worse, this persecution came to him simply because he had been faithful to God (10,15–17). Far from cursing his enemies, he has prayed for them (11), and this is his only reward. Worst of all, Yahweh does not seem to care: at least, he has done nothing to help (15). Has even God failed him (18)? The same temptation to despair and to give up his faith faced John in prison, as mentioned before (Matt. 11:2,3). Jeremiah was longing for reassurance. God's word was precious to him (16) but his suffering seemed to be endless, and he could not see why God did not bring it to an end, for Jeremiah always believed that God could (18).

Once again, God's 'comfort' is robust and uncompromising. He summons Jeremiah to return to his old position of faith and obedience (19), just as Jesus had told John that the man who did not lose faith in him was happy. Jeremiah stumbled over God's dealings with him, but God would not alter his way of dealing with him. Instead he would promise strength and safe keeping (20); but there can be no going back for Jeremiah (19).

TO THINK ABOUT: Was Jeremiah very 'unspiritual' to have such thoughts? Why did God not rebuke him? Why was it necessary for Jeremiah to suffer like this? Why are we constantly in danger of being 'offended' by Christ's demands, and of stumbling at his path for us? How do we overcome these difficulties?

16 Jeremiah's life-style a symbol

Jeremiah, as much as Hosea or Ezekiel, found that his own life-pattern was a picture to his contemporaries. A man of clinging affectionate nature, he was forbidden to have wife or children in Jerusalem (2). The reason lay in the emergency of the times: the siege was at hand, when wives and children would die like flies – this was no time to found a family (3,4). Similarly Paul, conscious of the imminent 'last days', warns against family ties in his age (1 Cor. 7:29,30, which may be a reminiscence of this present passage). But God's command goes further: Jeremiah may neither 'weep with those who weep' nor 'rejoice with those who rejoice' (Rom. 12:15). All these sorrows and joys shrank into insignificance compared with the magnitude of the coming disaster that is God's judgement (10).

What crime could possibly be great enough to merit such extreme punishment? God answers in terms that might come from Deuteronomy, probably the book rediscovered in Josiah's reign. It is because Judah has abandoned Yahweh, ignored his Law, and worshipped other gods (12). It was not a new crime: it was exactly what their ancestors had always done before them (11). So, since they have served foreign gods in Israel, they must now serve foreign gods in exile (13). This is the old law of 'tit for tat'. They cannot escape – God will send 'fishers' and 'hunters' to rout them out from wherever they have hidden (16). Yet, even here, there is a note of hope. The days will come when Israel will not only describe God as the God of the exodus, as they had done through all their history; they will also describe him as the God of the return from exile (14,15). When that happens, even the heathen nations will acknowledge God (19).

17 Blessings and curses

Ancient law codes often contained lists of blessings and curses as supplements. Deuteronomy chapters 27 and 28 give a good example from the Old Testament, and Luke 6:20–26, with its blessings and woes, is an example from the New Testament. For the reasons mentioned already, it is likely that Deuteronomy was in Jeremiah's mind in the present instance. It is, however, important to realise that, in the Bible, God's 'blessing' and God's 'curse' are seen as the inevitable results in God's world of two different attitudes to him. The words never contain the thought of impulsive arbitrariness that often exists in English usage. So the man who does not trust in Yahweh, but trusts instead in his fellow humans, has already put himself under a curse: he is bound to live his life in a 'desert' (6). Contrariwise, the man who trusts in Yahweh has a secret source of strength and hope, however difficult the circumstances: he has put himself in the situation where blessing is inevitable (8). The same things are said about Judah's observance (or non-observance) of the sabbath, since this denoted an attitude to God's gracious covenant (19–27), of which it was a sign.

These parts of the book of Jeremiah are so like some of the Psalms that two suggestions have been put forward. One is that men like Jeremiah were steeped in the Psalter; the other is that some of the later Psalms may actually have been written by the prophets themselves. Sometimes this general approach with universal 'rules' is compared with 'Wisdom Literature' in the Old Testament. Yet God, if dealing with generalities, will also deal with painful personal questions. To God, the human 'heart' (by which the ancient Hebrews meant the mind) is both devious and deceitful (9), and only God can plumb its depths.

18 The potter's house

This is one of the 'acted parables' of Jeremiah, by which God enabled him to make his meaning clear to his contemporaries. But he was only able to do this because God had first used the situation to make his plans clear to Jeremiah. Jeremiah is therefore only passing on the message that he has himself received. Unlike (say) Ezekiel, Jeremiah sees no bizarre vision. Instead, God shows him some common object, and makes him look at it with new eyes, so that it becomes a transparent medium for conveying deep spiritual truth. Here it is a potter's workshop, still one of the most familiar roadside sights in the villages of Asia (3). Pots are hand-made on the potter's wheel. If a particular 'throw' fails, the potter does not reject the clay. Instead, he simply remoulds the still malleable lump into another form, and makes a new pot (4). Nothing is irrevocable till the pot is fired in the kiln.

Nothing is irrevocable: that is the message for Judah, as well as for anxious Jeremiah himself. Both God's warnings of judgement (8) and his promises are conditional (10). This solves the problem of how some prophets could have been able to prophesy victory and success for Judah when only disaster came instead. It also solves the problem of what Judah can do now. True, Jeremiah is told to bring prophecies of judgement to Judah but, if Judah repents, these disasters need not be (11). The tragedy is that Judah stubbornly refuses to repent and so her judgement is sure (12). Nowhere in the world before has such a terrible thing ever been seen as Judah's abandonment of her God (13–16). That is why God will not move a finger to help her when the disaster comes (17). Lest we think this charge made by Jeremiah is unfounded, we have a particular instance in the stubborn, rebellious words of the people (18). Small wonder that Jeremiah prays as he does in 19–23, a prayer which reminds us of some of the Psalms, even if we may not use it today as Christians. But even this prayer springs from faith.

TO THINK ABOUT: What are the differences, if any, between the 'parables of Jeremiah' and the parables of Jesus? What other meanings does Paul find in this parable (Rom. 9:21)? Does the parable mean that God can change his mind? Has he only one plan for our life, or many?

19 The smashed jar

Like the chapter before, this acted parable begins with a command from God (1), the full meaning of which would only be clear to Jeremiah later. That it was to be a particularly solemn act is shown by the fact that Jeremiah took such weighty witnesses with him (1). These might have been warned of the nature of Jeremiah's message by the name of the gate by which they left the city (2). However, the name of 'Hinnom Valley' (2) conveyed nothing as yet, although (like similar places in other Semitic cities) it was sometimes called 'Topheth', meaning 'Ash-pit' or 'Fire-place' (6). This name was probably a reference to the altar-fires of Baal erected there, where firstborn sons were sacrificed as burnt-offerings (5). Because of this unthought-of sin, God will pour out his judgement on the place (3). So many will die that the valley will be called instead 'The Abattoir' (6) or 'Slaughter house'.

Jeremiah goes on to foretell a siege of Jerusalem so terrible that it will lead to open cannibalism of children (9). All men knew that such awful things had happened in a siege in Samaria long before (2 Kings 6:28): it was not a vain threat. But every prophet must give a sign; what sign would Jeremiah give? In one swift move, he smashed the new clay jar before the astonished witnesses (10) – smashed it ir-revocably into tiny useless fragments (11), saying that this was a symbol of the total destruction by God of city and state.

Once that has happened, there can be no mending. The whole of Jerusalem will be a 'Topheth', an 'ashpit', and the whole of the Valley of Hinnom will be a graveyard. Bad enough to proclaim such a terrible message at Topheth; but, at God's command, Jeremiah climbs up to the city again, and preaches the same words in the Temple itself (14). This, to the Judaean, would have been the ultimate sacrilege, and it is not surprising that it provoked a violent reaction from the priests.

Note: Pottery vessels were often used to store manuscripts or documents; they were sealed and buried, or deposited safely.

TO THINK ABOUT: What do you suppose the elders thought Jeremiah was going to do? What, in Israel, took the place of sacrificing the first-born? What theological truths does it teach us? Why did 'Gehenna' (the Valley of Hinnom) later become a picture of Hell?

20:1–6 False priest

Whatever a lunatic prophet might say or do on the town rubbish dump, certainly no one would tolerate what seemed like impudent blasphemy spoken in the name of the Lord in the Temple, least of all Pashhur, the priest in charge (1). So he had this unruly prophet beaten, and chained for the night in the Temple (2). Jeremiah was neither the first nor the last to suffer this fate for preaching God's word, as the apostles were to find (Acts 5:18,40). The next morning, Jeremiah was released (3); probably Pashhur thought that he would have learnt his lesson by now. But instead, Jeremiah had a new message from God, and he proclaimed it at once and fearlessly, though it might well have landed him back in chains again (3–6).

Symbolic names were commonly given in Old Testament days at particular crises in people's lives. Now, Jeremiah, in God's name, gives such a name to Pashhur. The first part of this name is a rhyming pun on his present name, as though his name were 'Fred', and God said: henceforth you will be called 'Dread'. And why was he to be so called? By his stubborn refusal to listen to God's word, he and the men like him were only hurrying God's doom on Jerusalem (4). He will live in dread himself, and others will run at the very sight of him (4). The whole fragile structure of Judah will collapse. The people will be slaughtered and the city plundered (5). When that happens, proud Pashhur and his noble priestly family will be among the wretched deportees dragged to Babylon. Irony of ironies, the priest who cared so much for Temple ceremonial will die and be buried in a ritually unclean land (6), surrounded in death by all his friends, who will realise too late that Pashhur had been telling them lies, and prophesying falsely in God's name.

TO THINK ABOUT: How does Jeremiah's experience in the Temple compare with that of Christ's? Why do religious people so often reject the word of the Lord? Why is it so serious to reject his word? Why was it necessary to make such an example of Pashhur? Does God always vindicate his servants in this life?

20:7–18 Jeremiah's complaint

There follows here one of Jeremiah's typical outbursts to God. Sometimes we must understand these merely as inspired records of Jeremiah's actual words, rather than something which we should copy. Verse 7 is like that: Jeremiah feels that God has cajoled and forced him into a false position, which only leads to his mockery by others (7,8). But Jeremiah is a true prophet. When he tries to be silent, and not to preach God's message, he cannot do it: preach it he must (9). That is what caused his dilemma. All around him, men and closest friends are involved in these plots, as Judas was to be involved in the arrest of Christ (John 13:18). We know that the men of his little priestly village of Anathoth were scheming against him (11:21), perhaps it is to them that he is referring here. Again, it is typical of Jeremiah (as of us) that his religious feelings ebb and flow. At one moment he is full of confidence, in the next he is full of despair! So in verse 11, his faith in God rises up to overcome this temptation. He knows that God will punish his enemies: indeed, he fervently prays for it (12). In this faith, he can even sing a song of praise (13).

But this elation does not last long. In a quick change, in a passage rich with imagery, he curses the very day he was born (14,15). Usually in Israel, the birth of a son was a time for blessing, but not the birth of Jeremiah whose whole life was to be full of trouble and sorrow (18). No, Jeremiah was not a happy man, and he did not have a happy life. But there are things far more important, both then and now, than a happy life, and faithfulness to God's word is one of them. It was not by accident that some of the contemporaries of Christ saw him as a second Jeremiah (Matt. 16:14), who, 'for the joy that was set before him, endured the cross, despising the shame' (Heb. 12:2).

TO THINK ABOUT: Was Jeremiah spiritually unstable, or just normal? Why does the Bible record outbursts like this? What spiritual value do they have for us? Does the Bible not promise to the follower of Christ a life of happiness? If not, what does God promise?

21–22:9 Judgement on the king

Zedekiah was not so much utterly wicked as weak, and his pious call to Jeremiah for prayer may not have been altogether hypocritical (2). But Jeremiah has, in any case, a terrible message for the royal army. It is not against Nebuchadnezzar alone that they fight, but against God himself (4). Jerusalem and its people will be destroyed and Nebuchadnezzar will have no mercy on the king and royal officials (7). But to the ordinary people, God gives a choice between life and death. If they stay in the besieged city, they will die, either in the fighting or by hunger and disease (9). If they desert to the Babylonians, they will remain alive. It was because of such outspoken prophecies that Jeremiah was later accused of treason, and even of attempting to desert to the Babylonians himself (Jer. 37:13). Jeremiah had learnt that patriotism is not enough.

Even at this eleventh hour there was still hope for the royal house (11,12), if only they would perform the traditional duty of the Davidic kings – to act justly and defend the wronged. If not, the fire would sweep all away (14), the fire that both symbolised and actualised God's anger. The hope for the royal house is outlined further in 22:1–3, in words reminiscent of the book of Deuteronomy that Jeremiah loved so much. If only they will rescue and protect the wronged, the helpless, the foreigner, the widow, the orphan – all those who have no man to help them and who must therefore depend on God – God will not only spare the kings but actually bless them (22:4) and even restore their old glory ('chariots and horses'). But if not, the palace at Jerusalem, dear as it is to God, will be hewn down like a cedar forest (7). What value will such destruction have? Wondering strangers will see the ruins of Jerusalem (8) and hear that this is the awful result of abandoning the true God for idols (9).

TO THINK ABOUT: Why was it hypocritical for Zedekiah to speak as he did (34:8–11)? Are Christians just as bound to care for the weak and helpless and oppressed? If so, why? If we do not, will God judge us as individuals or as a whole society? What relation has all this to eternal salvation?

22:10–30 Royal epitaphs

Here Jeremiah gives a set of pithy descriptions, usually far from complimentary, of the last few kings of Judah as God saw them, omitting Zedekiah with whom he has dealt already in the last chapter. He writes after Josiah's death (10). Josiah had been a good king, deeply committed to religious reformation; his death must have been a great blow to Jeremiah and was greatly mourned by the common people. Here, however, he tells the people not to mourn dead Josiah (10) but to mourn instead the boy-king who succeeded him, Joahaz or Jehoahaz, sometimes called Shallum (11). The Egyptians had swept him away at once into a royal captivity, from which he was never to return. Of all the later kings, he seems to have been the best: at least he is not castigated by Jeremiah.

On the other hand, of Jehoiakim (or Eliakim), Jeremiah's pet 'hate', he has plenty to say. Cynical and ruthless, Jehoiakim used the opportunity to line his own pockets dishonestly (13). He actually began to build himself a fine new palace in those awful days (14). If ever a man 'fiddled while Rome was burning', it was King Jehoiakim. He is scornfully contrasted with Josiah, his godly predecessor (15–17), who had fulfilled the dream of a just Davidic king (16) by 'saving' the poor and the innocent. What will the final result be? Proud King Jehoiakim will not even have the sort of royal funeral that Josiah had (18). In the confusion of the days leading up to the siege of Jerusalem, the king's body will be dragged away like carrion, and tossed outside the walls (19). No greater disgrace could ever befall any Israelite than to be thus unburied, dishonoured even in death.

As for Jehoiachin, Jehoiakim's son: God's signet-ring he might have been (24), but now he is as valueless as Jeremiah's smashed pot (28). He and his mother and his children must go into a hopeless exile without end (26), although, unknown to him now, there would be a ray of hope at the last (2 Kings 25:27).

Note: The 'signet-ring' was the sign of authority and thus something very precious to the owner.

TO THINK ABOUT: Why was Judah not to mourn the death of good King Josiah? Why was Shallum's fate worse than that of the exiles in Babylon? Why were Jehoiakim's crimes so terrible?

23:1–8 A ray of hope

God's judgement on the rulers of Judah has been proclaimed (1). Their chief crime is that they have utterly failed to fulfil their responsibility. Their task was to care for God's people: instead, like false shepherds they have destroyed and scattered the flock (2). The parallels to the Lord's words in John 10 are obvious. What will God do now? Have his plans been frustrated by wicked and careless men? For, after all, to punish the kings now will not save God's people from the scattering of exile. No: God has a deeper purpose that runs far beyond the exile. The exile is not the end, but only the beginning. God will bring the handful of exiles back home (3). Few in numbers though they are now, God will yet multiply them again. Greatest miracle of all, God will not abandon the marred pattern of kingship, but instead he will transform it by raising up righteous rulers (4) in place of the faithless kings of the past. This time, the king will be a true descendant of David (5), for he will rule with wisdom and justice, and under him the people will at last enjoy peace and safety (6).

As often, a symbolic name will be given to this coming king, 'The Lord our Righteousness' (a play on the name of the worthless King Zedekiah). This coming king will be all that Zedekiah was not. So great will be the joy of the return from exile that it will even overshadow in Judean minds the old miracle of the exodus (8). This, after all, was a new exodus in their own lifetime and experience. The exodus was, as we say today, 'actualised' for them. From now on, even the old event has a far deeper meaning.

We might note here that this 'new exodus' theme is repeated elsewhere in Jeremiah. No doubt, especially in the last days, he often reiterated the same subjects, and particularly the messages of hope.

23:9–40 God speaks to the prophets

There were three groups in Judah who had received from God the responsibility of caring for God's people: they were the kings, the priests, and the prophets. All these had failed, and Jeremiah condemns them all, in God's name. With Pashhur the priest he has already dealt in chapter 20:1–6; the kings have been listed and dismissed contemptuously in chapter 22; now, in this long chapter, it is the turn of the prophets to be rebuked. For, although Jeremiah was a prophet, he stood almost alone: the rest of his order, as we shall see, were 'false prophets'. Indeed, Jeremiah's greatest opposition came from the two groups of religious leaders, not from the civil power. The whole irony of the position is that these false prophets ought themselves to have been bringing God's word of warning to Judah, the word that might have saved her from judgement. Instead, Jeremiah must bring the same word of warning and judgement to them.

As before, Jeremiah would gladly have remained silent, but he could not (9). Even in the Temple itself, the heart of Israel's worship, prophet and priest are sinning (11). Samaria's prophets had led the Northern kingdom down to ruin by prophesying in Baal's name (13). The prophets of Judah are far worse, for they lead people astray in the name of the true God (13,14). To God, this means that Jerusalem is become as wicked as Sodom and Gomorrah, the old 'cities of the Plain' that God had destroyed utterly because of their sin (14). That means that the same doom will come to Jerusalem, and that any prophet who says anything else is a liar (18–20). God never sent such prophets (21): they never shared God's mind (22) or they would have proclaimed the true message that might have led to repentance. They preach their own empty dreams of success (27–32), not God's crushing word (29). When they stagger, burdened by disaster, into exile, they will know the truth – too late (38).

TO THINK ABOUT: Why was it that prophecy in Judah had fallen on such evil days? How can we know whether a prophet is really speaking God's words, or is 'false' (9,16,17)? Why have God's words such power (29)?

24 Two lots of figs

This is another vivid enacted parable of Jeremiah's, dated after the first captivity of 597 BC. In that year, to save destruction of the city, King Jehoiachin had surrendered to advancing Nebuchadnezzar and had been deported to Babylon, along with most of the 'key' persons of the shrunken state (1). However, the new King Zedekiah was left behind, and he and his contemporaries were totally unmoved by what had happened to Jehoiachin. Indeed, it seems as if they saw his captivity as a judgement from God, and their survival as a mark of God's special protection and favour. God was soon to disillusion them, through Jeremiah's word.

The two baskets of figs that Jeremiah saw outside the Temple (1) were genuine ordinary figs, probably intended for the presentation of first-fruits in the Temple. If that were so, the irony would be all the greater. Again, as in the fruit markets of today, one basket had beautiful early figs, always a special delicacy in Israel. The second basket, however, had rotten fruit (2) as Jeremiah's matter of fact reply to God points out (3). As usual, God then gives him a deeper insight as to the parable's spiritual meaning. Jehoiachin and his fellow deportees, so far from being under God's curse, are under his special protection and blessing (4–6). They are, in fact, the basket of choice figs. In exile, God will alter their hearts so that they will yearn to know God, and truly turn to him in penitence (7). In them, God will reiterate the great covenant promise: he will be their God, and they will be his people (7). This is the 'germ' of Jeremiah's great message about the new covenant of 31:31, which is finally realised only in the New Testament. But as for Zedekiah and his courtiers who remain – they are the rotten figs (8). They are, says God, a bad joke to the whole world (9). God has no future place for them in his purpose – could any punishment be worse?

25 Nebuchadnezzar, God's agent

Jeremiah's prophecies are not arranged chronologically: this is one that comes from the days of Jehoiakim, before Jehoiachin or Zedekiah even came to the throne. It is really an explanation of the divine strategy that lies behind all the events of the time and, in particular, the rise of Nebuchadnezzar and the Neo-Babylonian Empire. For this oracle is dated in Nebuchadnezzar's first year (1) and says bluntly that God has raised him up as his agent to punish stubborn Judah (9). Jeremiah points out that for all these years he has been bringing Judah the word of the Lord, but all to no purpose (3): Judah will not listen, and will not return to the Lord (4). So now there is no other way but that of punishment (9), a punishment which will leave Judah desolate and joyless (10). But God's punishment is both remedial and limited. Here, for the first time, we have mention of the 'seventy years' of servitude to Babylon (12). After that, God promises that even Babylon will be punished in its turn for its sins (12), and that all the prophecies of Jeremiah about it will be fulfilled, as were those about Judah (13).

This interpretation of history is common to all the great prophets of the Old Testament. God continually raises up heathen kingdoms, and uses these as instruments of judgement on his people (compare with Assyria in Isaiah 10:5) or agents of his will (e.g. Cyrus, in Isaiah 44:28). Equally, if they abuse their position, God puts such kingdoms down: Daniel 2:36–45 is an exposition at length of the same theme. Jeremiah explains that this is why God has made him a 'prophet to the nations' (1:10), with messages for all peoples of the known earth (15–25) and even, at the last, to Babylon itself (26). Especially, his word of warning is to the irresponsible 'shepherds' or leaders (34–36).

TO THINK ABOUT: Why did God use heathen nations to punish his own people? Was it fair first to raise up Babylon, and then to destroy her? Does God still act in this way in the affairs of nations? Why is 'Babylon' a symbol of evil in the New Testament? Does God still give us the ability to interpret his dealings with nations?

26 A second Shiloh

Shiloh, the ruined sanctuary of the Lord, lying in the territory of the old northern kingdom, was a name well known to every Israelite, for it dated back to the time of the undivided nation (Judg. 18:31) centuries before the Temple at Jerusalem was built. It had been God's chosen centre for all the tribes of Israel. Now, it was deserted and under a curse (Ps. 78:60). All men knew too why it had happened: it was because of the sin of Eli's family, traditional priests of the Lord there (1 Sam. 2). They also knew the awful warning of the event that had been brought by the youthful prophet Samuel to Eli (1 Sam. 3).

Now there was another prophet, bringing the same sort of warning, not to Shiloh, but to sacred Jerusalem itself (6). No wonder that priests, prophets and people alike were appalled and decided that he was a false prophet, and so should be put to death (8) as commanded in Deuteronomy (Deut. 18:20). They had no quarrel with what God had done to Shiloh. It had deserved its doom, they felt, but this was new Jerusalem, and things were different (9). Had not God chosen the holy city and appointed the site of the Temple and promised to live there? To them, its destruction was unthinkable, but they forgot that the men of Shiloh must have once said and thought the same. Fortunately for Jeremiah the death sentence must be pronounced by higher authorities than these, and so he was arraigned before the king's counsellors, the 'princes of Judah' (11). Jeremiah's sole defence was that he had spoken God's word (12), and his sole appeal was that they would repent (13) so that God might relent. The princes accepted his defence as valid (16) and quoted the parallel case of Micah, who had given a similar warning in Hezekiah's day (18). The only difference was that in those days Judah had responded (19). However, not every prophet was as fortunate as Jeremiah (20–23): others had to die for their faithfulness to God's word.

Note: At this time the 'princes of Judah' were the godly group of Josiah's men, the 'good figs' of the first captivity.

TO THINK ABOUT: Why were the priests and prophets so blind to the sin of Jerusalem? What message was there in this for the whole of Israel, God's chosen people (Rom. 11:17)? What message is there here for the Christian church (Rom. 11:22)?

27, 28 Bearing Nebuchadnezzar's yoke

This is a long prose passage (unlike most of Jeremiah, which is in verse) but it has one simple theme. God has appointed Nebuchadnezzar world ruler for the present, and all nations must submit to his yoke; otherwise they will only destroy themselves. This ran straight in the face of patriotism and national pride, but it was God's message, and so Jeremiah must preach it (3–6). Incidentally, as we look back now with historical hindsight, we can see that it was the truly wise course, but that is only what we would expect if it was indeed God's will. At the time, to all the small nations around, it seemed cowardly and unpatriotic madness, and so they rejected it.

Once again, Jeremiah was given a vivid enacted parable: he was to make a yoke and harness and wear them himself (2) as a symbol of acceptance of the authority of Nebuchadnezzar. Perhaps he was to send similar yokes to the kings of all the small countries around, allied with Zedekiah against Babylon (3). Certainly he was to send to them the interpretation of the parable (4–6), and the warning of the results of disobedience to God (8). This same warning was given to King Zedekiah (12–15) and the priests of Jerusalem (16–22). But a counter-prophet gave a counter-sign (28:1,2). Hananiah, one of the false prophets, broke the wooden yoke on Jeremiah's neck (10), and triumphantly said that this was God's symbol of breaking Nebuchadnezzar's yoke (4). Within two years, said he, Jehoiachin (sometimes called Jeconiah or Coniah) would return, and with him all the other exiles and the looted Temple vessels (3,4). But Jeremiah's response was that God would make a yoke of iron instead (13) and that Hananiah, not he, was the false prophet, and would die (16). So indeed it came about, within the year (17). Did the men of Judah heed the warning?

TO THINK ABOUT: Does a 'nationalistic' attitude belong more to the 'old man' than the 'new man' (Rom. 6:6; Eph. 4:22)? How can the Christian decide about such matters today? What guide-lines does the Bible lay down? What should our loyalties to our nation be now that we have no one particular 'chosen nation'? Are political questions like this as important to the Christian as to Israel in Old Testament days?

29 The letter to Babylon

Jeremiah dates this letter some time between 597 BC, the first deputation (when King Jehoiachin and the 'good figs' were taken into exile) and 586 BC, when Zedekiah and all the rest were swept away (2). Incidentally, it shows the free communication between Judah and Babylon during the period (3). This was probably because Judah was regarded at the time as just another province of the Babylonian Empire.

To the exiles, God sent a word of both comfort and warning. They were to settle down, work, marry, increase in numbers, and pray for the good of their captor-cities (5–7), since the future of the exiles was bound up with them. They were not to listen to the false prophets who (like Hananiah in 28:3) prophesied a quick and easy return from captivity (8) and the immediate return of the looted golden Temple vessels. True, God was commanding the exiles to settle down and multiply because it was his gracious purpose to bring them back again (14) but that would not be until after Babylon's seventy years of appointed rule (10), or, as put in 27:7, the days of Nebuchadnezzar, 'his son, and his grandson'. True, the Temple treasures taken with Jehoiachin would be returned, but again it would be in God's time (compare 27:22), not in the 'two years' specified by the false prophets. Indeed, before that happened, the rest of the Temple treasures would join them in Babylon. The 'bad figs' must first join the 'good figs' (17). The lying prophets in Babylon will suffer a terrible death at Nebuchadnezzar's hand (22): they will be burnt alive, not as martyrs but as criminals. As for Shemaiah, who wrote a 'counter-letter' to Jerusalem – his punishment will be to have no share in the return (32). He will not even live to see the blessings that God will give to his people.

Note: The Jews have always taken God's command given here as applying to all Jews of the Dispersion (5-7).

30–31:22 The promised return

So important is this message that Jeremiah is told to write it down (2), for God is going to bring his people back from exile, and restore to them their land (3). Many vivid metaphors are used: the people may be in labour-pains now, but that will pass away (5–7). The yoke and chains will be broken, but this time by God (8), and they will serve only God and a Davidic king (9). Now, Judah is desperately wounded (12). There is no cure for these wounds for God has inflicted them (15); but the God who punished will also heal (17). Is Jerusalem in ruins? It will be rebuilt, and the palace restored (18). Are they few in number now? They will be multiplied (19). Have they a foreign ruler now? Then, their prince will be a fellow countryman (21). The sheer joy of salvation will be so great that once again (like Miriam and the Israelite women of Exod. 15:20) the women will dance to the tambourine (31:4). The salvation will even spread to the hills of Samaria, lost to the invader a century and a half before (5). Indeed, the old bitterness between North and South will be swallowed up: men of Ephraim will once again come to worship at Jerusalem (6). The re-unification of North and South under a prince of the House of David had been a dream for centuries: now, the dream would become a reality.

Naturally, a song of praise follows (7–9), and God calls even the heathen to bear witness to what he is doing for his people (10). At the time of exile there was sorrow and crying. Jeremiah imagines Rachel, weeping in her tomb at Ramah for her descendants as they go into exile (15). But Rachel can dry her tears: they will return (16). The remaining verses are a loving exchange between God and his people (18–22), with a special thought in the last verse that will be developed later: God is about to do something completely new. He can in our lives too.

TO THINK ABOUT: Why was reunion between North and South under a Davidic king always part of the Israelite dream? What is the point of mentioning that the blind and lame and pregnant would share in this salvation? Why does the Bible stress that God can always do 'new things'?

31:23–40 The new covenant

It could be argued that this short passage is the heart of the whole book of Jeremiah, if not of the whole Old Testament. Certainly verses 31–34 hover on the verge of the New Testament, as does Isaiah 53. The Old Testament can take us no further. Yet we can see that this revelation from God was the only way out of the dilemma that Jeremiah had seen so clearly, and which caused him such anguish. How could sinful Judah ever change? And, if she could not change, how could God bring her back from exile? If he did, would she be any different? So, in verses 23–28, God once again reassures that he will restore the people. Indeed, each generation will have a new start with God, unburdened by the sins of the forefathers (29,30).

However, not even this is sufficient: a totally new type of covenant is needed, says God (31). For, no matter how great God's love, Israel always broke the old covenant (32). Israel herself must be inwardly changed. God's law must not be something external, but written into their very being (33). There will be no need for them to strive to teach their fellow countrymen to know God (as all the prophets had done), for this knowledge will be universal (34). Best of all, this will be a knowledge of the Lord as the one who forgives sins (34). It is on this basis that God will be Israel's God, and they will be his people (33). The great creator will never forsake them, whatever they do (35–37). It is on the basis of this promised new relationship that the further promise comes, that ruined Jerusalem will be built again (38–40).

Jeremiah dwells lovingly on the well-remembered familar details of the city, often obscure to us today. Best of all, even the defiled and cursed burial ground and rubbish dump of Jerusalem will be transformed into something sacred to God (40): the curse has at last been done away with.

32 Jeremiah's field

Dealing in real estate seems a strange occupation for a political prisoner in a besieged city; but this is what God called Jeremiah to do, as an act of faith in God's future. He was in jail for his prophecies against Jerusalem and against Zedekiah (3,4), even though they had been spoken at God's command. The Lord had already warned him of the impending visit of his cousin (6) so that it was no surprise when Hanamel came, requesting him to buy some family property in the village of Anathoth (8). Humanly speaking, it was pure madness: the Babylonian armies were ringing the city, and access to the property was only possible if they should withdraw temporarily (as in 37:11). Besides, if Jeremiah's prophecies came true, the city was about to fall, and the people were to go into captivity. What point was there in buying land at a time like this? Yet the Lord had told him to buy it, so buy it he did and, in so doing, Jeremiah gave another 'acted parable' of faith. By buying the land he showed his faith in God's word that the exile, inevitable though it was, was not to be the end of everything. God had said that after the return men should once again buy and sell land in Judah (15).

We have some very interesting practical details about the cost of a block of land at the time (9), and also about the registration of land-titles (10–12), but the chief interest is in the precautions for preservation of the title-deeds for a long time (14). But Jeremiah must still take his problems to God in prayer (16). He acknowledges both God's power and the justice of his punishment in Judah (17–23). He outlines the hard fact of the siege, and God's word that the city will fall (24): what sense does land-buying make (25)? Once again, God must gently and patiently reassure his troubled servant. God begins by agreeing with Jeremiah. It is true that judgement has been richly deserved and that judgement will fall on Judah (26–35). But it is equally true that God will restore the exiles, make an eternal covenant with them (40), and that land will be bought and sold, even in tiny Benjamin, Jeremiah's home area (44).

Note: We probably have here an example of the Israelite custom of redemption of family property. See Ruth 4:3 for another example.

33 David, Levi, and Jerusalem

In Jeremiah's early ministry, when men believed that Jerusalem would never fall, their hearts were proud and hard, so that Jeremiah actually had to bring words of judgement. Now it seems that the disaster has begun to fall, and Jeremiah must bring words of encouragement, for fear that they may lose heart altogether. God assures Jeremiah first of his almighty power to act (2) and then of his will to act in unthought-of ways (3). True, he will destroy Jerusalem (4,5) but he will also rebuild it (6–9). People are right to say that it is like an empty desert now (10), for God never ignores the present reality of our situation – but it will yet be filled with happy crowds (11).

Three signs will be given to prove the reality of his working. First, Jerusalem will be so changed in nature that she will receive a new symbolic name, 'The Lord our righteousness' (16). This is possibly also a pun on the name of the old priest-king of pre-Israelite Jerusalem, Melchizedek: 'My King is Righteousness' (Gen. 14:18), remembering that, in the Old Testament, 'righteousness' includes the idea of 'salvation'. Second, there will always be a descendant of David sitting on the throne (17). Third, there will always be priests from the tribe of Levi to offer sacrifice (18). This was important to every Israelite, since God's covenanted word in the past to David and to Levi's tribe was involved (21). This was a covenant as sure as that which assures that evening and morning follow each other (20). People outside Israel were saying (24) that God had rejected the two families he had chosen, and with whom he had made a covenant (either Israel and Judah, or David and Levi, or Israel and David: but it makes little difference). But when they saw how God would continually choose one of David's descendants to rule over Israel, they would know that God had kept his covenant in history (26) as he had in nature (25), and that he can be trusted completely.

34 Freedom for slaves

King Zedekiah was weak, but not absolutely wicked, and so Jeremiah would still bring messages from God to him. This was a message of encouragement, although it may not seem very encouraging to us. Zedekiah would not die in battle: he would be taken as prisoner to Babylon, die there in peace, and be mourned as a king should be (1–6). At least he would escape Jehoiakim's fate of being carrion for the dogs outside Jerusalem (22:19). But the king's utter worthlessness is seen in his acquiescence in the deceitful treatment by their masters of the Hebrew slaves in Jerusalem (8,11). In their extremity, which they knew to be the result of God's anger, they remembered the old law of Deuteronomy 15:12 enjoining the freeing of enslaved fellow-Hebrews after seven years (14). In their anxiety to please God (15) they determined to revive and keep this apparently long-neglected law. So the people agreed to free Israelite slaves, and did actually do it (10), making a solemn covenant to do so in the Temple (18). They even revived the archaic form of oath-taking found in Gen. 15:9–17, the most solemn oath of all. A sacrificial animal was cut in two and the parties to the oath filed between the severed parts. This was an 'acted prayer' that, if they did not keep the oath, God would do the same to them as they had done to the animal. But they were guilty on this occasion of the most terrible duplicity. They agreed to this right action in a moment of danger; when the danger had temporarily receded, they changed their mind, and went back on their covenant (16). Such treachery is almost unbelievable. We can imagine what utter despair must have filled the hearts of the slaves after the brief joy of freedom. Worst of all, God had commanded Israel to act in this way to their slaves because it was the way that God had acted to them, in freeing them from Egypt's slave-pen (13). Such men can have had no knowledge or experience of God's salvation themselves: they therefore must suffer the fate of covenant breakers, the fate that they themselves had mimed (19–22) in the oath-taking.

TO THINK ABOUT: How could the Judeans be so treacherous and heartless? Why is it that our attitude to others reveals our attitude to God? Was God just in his dealing with Judah and Jerusalem? What does this passage say to us in our world today?

35 The faithfulness of the Rechabites

God wants to bring home, by a living parable, the extent of the unfaithfulness of Judah towards him. He will do this by leading Jeremiah to point out the consistency and faithfulness of a group of ordinary individuals within Judah to a far less solemn bond than God's covenant. Sometimes the marriage-bond is chosen by the prophets as an illustration of faithfulness; here the example comes from the group called the Rechabites, named after a distant ancestor. Their ancestor had been a stubborn old man, who refused to change with the times (6,7). He was doubtless used to the wilderness life, and held that no good could come of the new Canaanite farming methods – ploughing fields and planting vineyards. As for houses, he despised them: true Israelites lived in tents, like their patriarchal fathers.

We have all met aggravating old men like that, and Jeremiah does not say that his views were correct, however sincerely held. But his was a private protest against a corrupt, affluent society like that of those who choose an 'alternative life-style' today. There were other groups who made similar protests on religious grounds: the Nazarites, for instance, would neither cut their hair nor drink wine; the prophets, till quite a late date, still obstinately wore woven hair cloaks. But Jonadab, son of Rechab, not only held their views himself, but, like many a patriarch, tried to insist that his family held them too (6,7). The miracle was that, presumably because of the commandment to honour parents (Exod. 20:12), they obeyed (8–10). Jeremiah was told to test their obedience by inviting them in for a drink (1–5). Their leader patiently explained that they could not drink wine (never itself considered wrong by Israelites) because of this binding commandment of their ancestor. But Judah had consistently disobeyed the command of a far greater one; so God would punish Judah and reward the Rechabites (16–19).

Note: Wine was probably avoided by these groups both because of its fermentation (understood by them as putrescence) and also because it was characteristic of the life of Canaanites, not of wilderness life.

TO THINK ABOUT: Were the Rechabites either correct or effectual in their protest? If not, did their protest have any value? Does God reward faithfulness to human obligations? If so, why? What protest, if any, are Christians called to make today by their life-style?

36 The reading of the scroll

This is an interesting chapter because it helps us to understand how the originally spoken words of the prophets were written down and preserved in books as we have them today. Here, God tells Jeremiah to write down all his past prophecies (compare 30:2) in the hope that their collective force will cause Judah to repent (2,3). It also shows us that sometimes, at least, prophets had secretaries (4): Baruch wrote, while Jeremiah dictated (compare Rom. 16:22). Now it had to be read: the Temple, thronged with worshippers on a ceremonial fast day, would be ideal (6). Probably, the day of fasting was an attempt to win God's favour in view of the coming Babylonian attack. For some reason Jeremiah was debarred from the Temple attendance, so Baruch read it aloud for him (8). But not for long: the words were too inflammatory. Baruch was fetched before the Council of Nobles (still the 'good figs' at this date) and asked to read the scroll to them (15). Appalled, they decided that the king must have this solemn message from God (16), having first checked the credentials of the scroll itself (17). However, they were obviously apprehensive about the reception of such a message by King Jehoiakim, so they prudently urged both Baruch and Jeremiah to go into hiding until the results were known (19).

Verse 22 is the vivid touch of an eyewitness: it was winter, and the king was sitting by a brazier. It also explains what the king did later. As the scroll was read to him column by column, he contemptuously slashed them off, and tossed them into the brazier (23), careless of the protests of the group of godly nobles (25). As they had guessed, the king ordered the arrest of Baruch and Jeremiah, but in vain (26). But Jehoiakim could neither silence the word of God nor impede its outcome. Jeremiah is commanded to write another scroll (28), and God pronounces his judgement on Jehoiakim and his courtiers, and all who despise God's word (31).

TO THINK ABOUT: How would Jeremiah have remembered all his past prophecies? What was God's continual purpose for his people in sending his servants the prophets? Were these 'temple fasts' pleasing to God or not (9)? Why was there no hope for Jehoiakim?

37 Jeremiah's imprisonment

It says a great deal for the status of a prophet in Israel (compare 26:19) that, although Jeremiah may have been beaten and put in the stocks overnight (20:2), he had not yet been imprisoned permanently. Even now, his charge was a political rather than a religious one (13). The chapter begins with wavering King Zedekiah asking Jeremiah for prayer (3), though he was not prepared to obey God's word (2). Things looked brighter: a relieving army from Egypt had temporarily lifted the Babylonian siege of Jerusalem (5). But Jeremiah warns Zedekiah that this is only a temporary respite (7). The Babylonian army will return and burn Jerusalem, as God had said (8–10), even if they only had 'walking wounded' left to fight for Babylon. Jeremiah, however, tried to take advantage of the temporary respite, probably to visit the plot of family land that he had recently bought at Anathoth in Benjamin (12). Not surprisingly, he was recognised and arrested by the sentries at the city gate on a charge of attempted desertion which, of course, he denied (14). But it is hard to blame the sentry for a very natural conclusion: after all, Jeremiah had consistently urged others to desert (21:9). That was the irony: men simply regarded Jeremiah as pro-Babylonian and unpatriotic. Once again, Jeremiah came before the princes (14) for trial.

By now, they were the 'bad figs'; the 'good figs' had been taken into exile with King Jehoiachin. So Jeremiah was beaten and imprisoned, and might indeed have died, had not weak King Zedekiah intervened. The king wanted a secret interview with Jeremiah (17), as Nicodemus had with Jesus. But it did the king little good, for the message of disaster was always the same. That is the origin of the English expression 'a Jeremiad' which describes a gloomy complaint, although it is not very fair to Jeremiah. But at least Zedekiah moved him to 'loose confinement' in the barracks, and gave him a daily ration (21). Apparently, Zedekiah did not dare to free him. Like Pilate, he was too conscious of the cost of doing right.

TO THINK ABOUT: Why was Zedekiah so weak? Is a person like that to blame? Was Jeremiah really 'pro-Babylonian'? If so, why? In what sort of areas might a Christian have to suffer unpopularity today?

38 Ebed-Melech, the Ethiopian

Whatever King Zedekiah thought, the princes (all hard and ruthless men now) had decided that Jeremiah must die. With his defeatist prophecies he was a security risk, and was undermining morale (4). Again, they were right from their point of view. That is exactly what Jeremiah was doing, but he was doing it on God's express orders (2). Those who oppose God's word are always driven, step by step, to more extreme measures: they must try to silence God's messenger at all costs (compare John 11:48–50). King Zedekiah weakly confessed his own helplessness before them (5) so they triumphantly seized Jeremiah, and lowered him into an empty water-cistern, whose bottom was thick with mud (6). Whether they hoped that he would drown in the mud or starve to death, their plan was clearly to kill him. But, while Zedekiah was afraid to help and the princes were unwilling to help, a black slave of the king risked his life to help Jeremiah (7).

Ebed-Melech's name simply means 'King's Slave', and it is probable that he was just that – a Nubian royal slave, possibly a court eunuch, in view of his position and influence. His bold and simple intercession with the king certainly saved Jeremiah's life (9,10), for it was typical of this weak king that he would respond to the pressure of the moment. Ebed-Melech was not only courageous, but also practical: it was not the first time that he had used ropes to rescue men from sucking mud (11–13). Timorous Zedekiah again sought from Jeremiah the counsel that he was afraid to take (14); but this time Jeremiah is more cautious (15). Given royal reassurances, Jeremiah brings the same mind from God as before. It is interesting to note that, even at this late date, the destruction of Jerusalem could have been avoided by one man's obedience, an obedience which he was afraid to give (17–23). So back Jeremiah went to the Court of the Guard, this time under a vow of secrecy (24), but sure of royal protection.

TO THINK ABOUT: What was the basic error of the princes, from which all else flowed? Why did Ebed-Melech act as he did? Did God know in advance which way Zedekiah would decide? Was it right for Jeremiah to deceive the princes as he did?

39 The fall of Jerusalem

Here at last is the climax up to which the whole book has been leading: the great walls of Jerusalem are breached (2). There is a roll call of the grim Babylonian generals as they sit in state in the conquered city (3), names which conjured up vivid images to the Judaeans. But meanwhile Zedekiah and his troops had burst out, making for the safety of the hills in the south (4). Too late: the Babylonian troops caught up with them at Jericho, where Zedekiah was captured and his troops scattered (5). Zedekiah was brought as prisoner and oath-breaker to Nebuchadnezzar's campaign headquarters at Riblah, far to the north (5). God's word to Zedekiah through the prophet Jeremiah (32:4) came true in every detail, but in an ironical way. He did indeed speak face to face with Nebuchadnezzar, and see him eye to eye: but first he saw his sons killed and then the princes of Judah who had led him astray. Finally, he himself was blinded, and taken in chains to Babylon (7), while the city of Jerusalem was burnt and the walls broken down (8). All the survivors, whether deserters or not, were then deported to Babylon (9) except for a few landless peasants, left to care for the land.

What thoughts went through the mind of the blinded king, as he stumbled his way to Babylon? The end of this weak man was almost worse than that of a wicked man like Jehoiakim for, in the case of Zedekiah, there was always the 'might have been'. But there are two rays of hope even in this dark chapter. The first deals with Jeremiah: the Babylonians paid special attention to caring for him (11–14), since they probably regarded him as leader of the pro-Babylonian party. The second is that, even on this dark day, God did not forget Ebed-Melech (15–18). As always, faith was rewarded by God, and unbelief was punished.

TO THINK ABOUT: Why did Nebuchadnezzar treat Zedekiah so cruelly? Was it significant that Judah was cleansed of all but the poor and helpless? Would the fulfilment of God's word of judgment now give the exiles confidence that he would fulfil his word of promise too?

40, 41 Gedaliah at Mizpah

Terrible though the climax was, there are two acts still to come, taking the tragedy still further. The Babylonians had given the choice to Jeremiah either of coming to Babylon, where he would be treated with honour, or remaining behind in the ruined country (4). Not surprisingly, Jeremiah chose the latter course, and was entrusted to the care of Gedaliah, a Judean noble whom Nebuchadnezzar had made Governor of the province of Judah (5). He was a descendant of a godly house that had supported Jeremiah, and had his headquarters at Mizpah, since Jerusalem was uninhabitable. Gradually, a pathetic remnant of Judah gathered round Gedaliah there – bands of roving soldiers, refugees returning from neighbouring countries, landless peasants and so on (7–12). He encouraged them to submit to Babylon, and to collect the grapes and other fruit ripening in the empty fields of Judah.

It looked as if a tiny commonwealth loyal to God might continue, but it was not to be. Those who had stubbornly rejected God's word before were still set on the collision course that would destroy even this tiny remnant. This time the agent was Ishmael (14), a minor member of the royal family (41:1) who probably considered Gedaliah both an upstart and a traitor. Gedaliah had been warned about Ishmael but was too honest a man to believe the story (40:16). First, Ishmael treacherously murdered Gedaliah and his Babylonian bodyguard (41:2,3); then he wantonly murdered a group of northern pilgrims coming to mourn the sack of the Temple (4–8). Finally, he decamped in the direction of Ammon, with the rest of the Judean remnant as prisoners or hostages (10). Retribution soon overtook him: the Judean soldiers caught up with him, defeated him, and freed the joyful prisoners (11–14). But what were the wretched remnant to do now? They paused, near Bethlehem, to consider their position (17): Judah's fate hung in the balance.

TO THINK ABOUT: Was the sack of Jerusalem not enough? Why did God allow this new disaster to happen? How does it show that the heart of the Judeans was still unchanged? Why are men of integrity, like Gedaliah, always at a disadvantage in this world?

42, 43 The last chance

In this time of disaster Johanan, the army commander, with the other leaders, quite rightly turned to Jeremiah to ask for a word from the Lord to guide them (1–3). That showed a right spirit, as did the way in which they swore in advance to obey God's command whether acceptable to them or not (5,6). Jeremiah took time and prayer to ask for God's guidance: it was ten days before he summoned them for an answer (7). After all that waiting, were they disappointed? The word was nothing new, but 'the same old thing'. God told them not to fear, to remain in the land, and to submit to the king of Babylon: if they did that, God would bless them (9–12). It was so simple, and yet so profound. It was the response of faith. Of course, God (and Jeremiah) knew well that there was really only one alternative to this: they would cross the border and flee to Egypt, as they had already considered doing (41:17). So, in case they were still tempted to move in this direction, God warned them of the inevitable results (13–18). Jeremiah added his own pleadings (19–22), reminding them of their promise to obey the Lord's command, however unpalatable.

He must have had more than an inkling of what was going to happen: Jeremiah was dealing with men who had already made up their minds. So Johanan and his friends flatly rejected this counsel (43:4) and, worse still, accused Jeremiah of lying in bringing it (2). Why Baruch was blamed for it all, we cannot say (3): any excuse is good enough for stubborn men. So they went down to Egypt, taking Jeremiah with them. But even there, by acted parable, Jeremiah showed that there was no safety outside the will of God (8–13); and no escape from God's judgement except in repentance and obedient faith.

44 When Israel was in Egypt

Israel's great day of salvation was when she had been delivered from Egypt at the exodus. She had no greater horror than the thought of returning to Egypt (see Deut. 17:16). Yet here the remnant of Judah had done it of their own accord (12); they had deliberately put the clock back. But although God still speaks (2), if Johanan and his friends had not listened in Judah, they were not likely to listen in Egypt. Jeremiah reminds them of how idolatry and unfaithfulness to their God had already led to the disaster of Jerusalem (1–6). Why then do they do exactly the same things in Egypt (8)? None of them, except a tiny handful, will now share in the joy of the return when that great day comes (14). We live in a day when the rights of women are stressed. It was the women who answered Jeremiah on this occasion, possibly because they outnumbered the men among the refugees; possibly because the domestic (as distinct from Temple) worship concerned them more directly. Their reply was blunt and dramatic: they finally and utterly refused to listen to God's word (16). They would continue to burn incense to the 'Queen of Heaven' (17), as they defiantly said their ancestors had done. Indeed, they said that it was only when they ceased worshipping her (presumably in the days of Josiah's reforms) that their troubles had started (18). Further, their men stood solidly with them in this (15,19). To such stubbornness, Jeremiah says there can only be one answer – disaster (26–28); and the overthrow of Pharaoh Hophra would be a sign (30).

Note: The worship of the Queen of Heaven was a typical Babylonian star-cult.

TO THINK ABOUT: Why did the refugees seem bent on their own ruin? Had they learnt nothing from God's judgement on Jerusalem? Why was the worship of the Queen of Heaven so attractive to them? Where was the flaw in their analysis of history?

45 Comfort for Baruch

This tiny chapter is pathetic in a way because it is comfort, and also gentle rebuke, to a faithful friend. We know that Baruch was a scribe, and thus quite an important man. We also know that he had written out the scroll for Jeremiah, at the latter's dictation (36:4). On him alone, without the help of Jeremiah, had fallen the dangerous task of reading the scroll to the hostile crowds in the Temple (36:10). He had had to appear before the Court of the Princes for the investigation (36:14–18), and he, like Jeremiah, had had to go into hiding. It was as well for him that he did: he, with Jeremiah, was on King Jehoiakim's 'wanted' list (36:26).

We do not know what had happened in the years that followed. That he had been a faithful friend and continuing supporter of Jeremiah is clear from Johanan's remark in 43:3. Baruch, too, was regarded as a coward and a traitor – indeed, to judge from this passage, even more so than Jeremiah himself. That is the clearest proof of his faithfulness to God; and yet this passage shows that it was not a faithfulness which came easily. This prophetic word was given to Jeremiah for Baruch in the fourth year of Jehoiakim (1), the very year of the scroll-writing and reading (36:1). Baruch (like Jeremiah at times) was ready to give up (3). It seems as if, deep in his heart, he still had the secret hope that, without being unfaithful to God, he might obtain a great place for himself as a scribe, perhaps in royal service. So he is warned not to seek great things for himself (5), but simply to continue in obedience. When God himself is destroying, with a breaking heart, what he most loves (4), is that a time for Baruch to be thinking of himself? But even in the midst of the shaking of all things, Baruch (like Ebed-Melech in 39:18) can be sure of God's protection (5). That will be his only reward, but it will be more than sufficient.

TO THINK ABOUT: How is it that Jeremiah, sorely tempted to despair himself, could yet comfort others tempted to despair (2 Cor.1: 3–7)? Was it wrong of Baruch to want to be great in God's service? Why did God not give him (or Jeremiah) a greater reward? How was this oracle preserved?

46 Message for Egypt

Jeremiah had been called to be a 'prophet to the nations' (1:5). So far, we have seen a few of his 'international prophecies', but only those dealing with Judah. Now, chapters 46 to 51 are a sort of appendix of oracles addressed to other countries, not necessarily in chronological order, covering both the great imperial powers and Judah's tiny fellow nations. This first oracle (3–12) was clearly written when Pharaoh Neco's troops were marching north with high hopes to deal with the unknown Babylonian general, Nebuchadnezzar, commanding the army of his father Nabupolassar. Egypt was a proud ancient military power (3,4), attacking swiftly like the Nile in flood (7,8), with men from every corner of Africa (9). But in a vision, God shows Jeremiah this splendid army falling over itself in shameful defeat (6,12). Worse will follow (14–24): Jeremiah vividly portrays a Babylonian counter-attack, and a subsequent attack on Egypt (though the invasion and conquest only came in its fullness during the Persian Empire, a century later).

Panic reigns in the centres of northern Egypt where the Judeans had fled (14). Their calf-god Apis is helpless to protect them now (15). Egypt is given a new derisive name, for she is all talk and no action, living in past glories. The explanation lies in the oracle in 25, 26: God is punishing both Amon, the great god of Egypt, and proud Pharaoh, its king. But, characteristic of Jeremiah, the promise is given that even for Egypt there will be forgiveness and restoration. If Judah can be forgiven, so can Egypt (26). So, hard on this, comes the great promise to God's people: they will be brought home in peace (27,28). Nothing else matters in comparison with that.

TO THINK ABOUT: Why are some prophecies fulfilled almost immediately, and others only centuries later? Does it affect their respective truth? How did Jeremiah get these messages to the other countries? Does his book give us any hints (27:3; 51:61)? Do you suppose that they heeded God's words? If not, why tell them?

47 God's word to the Philistines

The Philistines (who gave their name to Palestine) had been a roving sea-faring people from Crete (4), who settled on the coast of Canaan shortly after Israel had occupied its hill country, and fought Israel to a standstill till David finally conquered them (2 Sam 5:17–25). They were professional soldiers and their fine fortress cities were still a power in the coastal plain. In this period, they were one of the coalition of small powers, usually headed by Judah, that opposed the great empires of the day – now Egypt, and now Babylon. The attack on the fortress of Gaza by the chariots is compared to a flood that nothing can stop (2,3). Why is the flood irresistible? Because God's time to destroy the Philistines has come (4), and it is of no use appealing to him to sheath his sword until the task is done (6,7). No sword forged against Israel will prosper (Is. 54:17); but this is the 'sword of the Lord' drawn against Philistia. Today, the old Philistine cities are barren sand dunes by the Mediterranean coast: the cities that bear their names are new Israeli settlements nearby. And why? The Philistines, a non-Semitic people, are always described in the Old Testament as 'uncircumcised' (Judg. 14:3); they do not bear on their bodies the mark of God's covenant. We use the word 'Philistine' to mean 'uncultured', but the Philistines were a wealthy warrior-aristocracy, rich in the culture of their day. The Bible sees them instead as a proud self-confident people, trusting in the armaments of the world instead of in God (1 Sam. 17:45). That was why their downfall was inevitable.

TO THINK ABOUT: Was God cruel to destroy a refugee people like the Philistines? What does the sin of the Philistines say to us today? Had God been in control of all Philistine history as he was in control of Israelite history (Amos 9:7)? Does he control all world history today? What then was special about Israel's history?

48 What of Moab?

Moab had been a sister-people of Israel, with common patriarchal links (Gen. 19:37). Even David had some Moabite blood in his veins (Ruth 4:17), and his parents had actually stayed with the king of Moab while he was 'on the run' from Saul, although David fought and conquered Moab later (2 Sam. 8:2). But ever since wilderness days, when the Israelites became ensnared in the immoral Baal-worship of Moab (Num. 25:1), Moab had been an enemy. She too was, from time to time, a member of the pathetic little confederacy that tried in vain to oppose God's will as experienced in the raising-up of Nebuchadnezzar (Jer. 27:3). Jeremiah warned in vain; now, the judgement must fall on them.

In verses 1 to 5 a succession of Moab's cities is named, pictured as falling one by one to the invader. There is an irony in verse 6: they are to run from the enemy like their own onager, the wild donkey of the arid steppes of Moab. The reason for the disaster is given in verse 7: Moab trusted in her strength and wealth. She trusted in Chemosh her god; now Chemosh and his priests must go into exile together. In all the secure past of Moab, this sort of mass displacement had never happened before (11). Now their ultimate disaster will come, so that they will be as disillusioned with Chemosh as Israel is with her false idols (13). There follows a typical burial dirge (14–20), the meaning of which is explained afterwards in prose (21–39). Added to their old sin of pride (29) was the sin of mocking God's people in the day of their disaster (27), when a brother would have sympathised. Moab, too, has fulfilled Jeremiah's symbolism of the smashed pot (38,39). Henceforth, Moab is smashed, useless, unwanted; and as she mocked God's people, so others will mock her (39). But even for Moab, God in his mercy will give a ray of hope in the future (47).

TO THINK ABOUT: Why does God give hope even to Egypt and Moab, the enemies of his people? Is it because of his nature? Had he a plan of salvation for them too? If so, what was 'salvation' in Old Testament days, and how could they obtain it? What was Israel's place in this? Had she fulfilled her role or not?

49 Ammon, Edom, and the rest

The rest of the members of the coalition all receive in turn from the Lord their message of condemnation, sometimes short, sometimes longer. For Ammon, there are the pithy words of 1–6 only. Ammon has seized the opportunity of Israel's captivity to occupy the land of the tribe of Gad (1). Rabbah, the Ammonite capital, must fall, so that Israel can regain her lost territory (2). They trust in Milcom, their god: very well – Milcom (or his statue) must go into exile like the priests and princes of Moab (3). Yet Ammon too will be made prosperous again one day (6).

Edom has a longer condemnation (7–22), but the pattern is the same. They were once famous for their wise men; where have they gone now? (7). Edom was Esau's descendant (8), proud in their inaccessible cliff-fortress of Sela ('the Rock'), called 'Petra' today (16). Even from there, the Lord will bring them down. Their destruction will be as complete as that of Sodom and Gomorrah (18).

Damascus, one of the oldest cities of the area, is dismissed in verses 23–27. Her sister-cities in the north will be terrified when they hear the news (23). The once-popular trading city will be deserted (25) and, in the general conflagration, the wealthy palace of Ben-Hadad will be burnt to the ground (27), all on the authority of the word of the Lord.

Kedar (a nomadic Arabian tribe) and Hazor, a desert city, will fare the same (28–32). The tents and camels of the nomads will be seized, and the city will be left a ruin where desert foxes yelp (33). Elam, a northern neighbour of Babylon, may once have been famous for her archers, but her people will flee as refugees to every conceivable country (36) – until the day comes when God will restore them (39). So ends the once proud coalition against God.

TO THINK ABOUT: How would you explain Deut. 2:19, where God says he will not give Ammon's land to anyone else? Is the 'exile of Ammon' a contradiction of this? If Edom is to be treated like this, what has become of the blessing to Esau? (Gen. 27:39, 40)? Do you see any similarities between Esau and his descendants? Are all God's promises conditional on our reponse?

50 God's word to mighty Babylon

So far, we have only had God's judgement on the nations who have opposed his will in opposing Nebuchadnezzar of Babylon. But Jeremiah had always insisted that Babylon's time was limited, and that God would judge her too (27:7). Now at last comes the detailed proclamation of her doom although the city was only to fall unscathed, long after Jeremiah's death, into the hands of Cyrus the Persian (2 Chron. 36:20–23) and be destroyed under one of his successors. When Babylon fell, the news would spread like wildfire among her subject peoples (2). Merodach, the great god of Babylon, would be shamed for evermore: the 'nation from the north' (3) – Persia – would conquer her. The 'making of Babylon into a desert' was only fulfilled long afterwards: but certainly it is abundantly true today. But the initial fall of Babylon would be the joyful signal for the exiles to return (4,8).

Nebuchadnezzar and his people would be punished for their cruelty to God's people (17,18), just as Assyria had been punished before them for the same reason. Even more, they would be punished for their pride against Israel's God (29). Pride, that oldest of human sins, had been the downfall of Babylon (31): the Persian cavalry and archers would bring them down (42). When great Babylon falls, the very earth will shake and resound (46). She is not like one of the little nation-states whose downfall has been predicted in the previous chapters. Perhaps that is one reason why the fall of Babylon has become in the New Testament a symbol for 'the last great battle' when all human world powers come crashing down at last before the power of God (compare Rev. 18). The most significant item in the dirge of 35–38 is the condemnation of the lying prophets and deceiving idols of Babylon (36,38); the truth overtakes all mankind at the last.

TO THINK ABOUT: Can you think of four reasons why Babylon (rather than, say, Assyria) should have so often been used as a symbol of evil and opposition to God in later days? Once again, does the time-lag between the fulfilments of the two halves of the prophecy have any significance? Why is prophecy so often 'timeless' or 'foreshortened'? If Babylon was to fall, why were the false prophets wrong to foretell its fall (28:15 etc.)?

51 Babylon continued

This chapter, along with renewed prophecies of the fall of Babylon, contains more and more urgent warnings to the exiles who are present in her to flee, lest they too be involved in her destruction. God has already issued this call in 50:8; it is reiterated in verses 6, 45 and 50 of this present chapter. Like Lot fleeing from Sodom, they are to run for their lives (Gen. 19:17).

In the New Testament, this becomes the urgency to respond to the gospel, and thus to escape the universal judgement that is to fall on the world. Since Babylon becomes a symbol of evil world-power in the New Testament (e.g. Rev. 17:5), it is not surprising that other symbols used here (like the golden drinking-goblet that brings drunkenness to the nation, verse 7) are also found in Revelation (Rev. 17:4;18:3). Indeed, without some knowledge of the Old Testament prophets, it is impossible to understand the symbolism of the book of Revelation.

The chapter also makes earlier prophecies more specific: what in 50:3 and 41 were 'strong nations in the north' have now become specifically 'the kings of Media' (11,28), while 27 lists many of the tribes in the north who supplied contingents to the Persian army. A solemn psalm of praise to God the creator is called forth by this consideration of his doings (15–19), and one of the clearest statements of God's purposes for Babylon (20): see Isaiah 10:5 for a very similar description of Assyria in an earlier day.

The chapter ends with the record of yet another 'acted parable' of Jeremiah. At the Lord's command, Jeremiah wrote down all his prophecies against Babylon (60) and entrusted them to a royal emissary going to Babylon, with instructions to read them aloud to any who would listen. Then, the scroll was to be tied to a stone, and sunk in the Euphrates – just as Babylon would sink, never to rise again (64).

TO THINK ABOUT: Why did so many Judeans remain behind in Babylon even after the liberation when the exiles returned home? What was the greatest danger in Babylon? Of what was the Lord warning them? Were Jeremiah's prophecies about Babylon designed to encourage the exiles, or to warn the Babylonians to repent? Can you see any similarities to the book of Jonah, and God's attitude to Nineveh shown there (Jon. 4:11)?

52 The end of the matter

This is a virtual repetition, with further details, of the events recorded in chapter 39, almost identical with 2 Kings 24 and 25, from which it may have come. In verses 17–23, one can hear the agony of a godly Judaean, recounting in detail all the sacred Temple treasures that were taken away by the Babylonians. It must have been a priest who recorded the details of the measurements of the columns and the sheer size of the bulls, the tank, etc. After all, Jeremiah was a priest himself (1:1), although from Anathoth and therefore probably from Eli's line and so debarred from service in the Temple. The information as to the names and numbers of the deportees could only have come from a contemporary document (24–30). The surprising thing to us is that the actual numbers are so small: but the population of Jerusalem was doubtless already greatly reduced by war and famine.

If the book were to end like this, it would end on a note of tragedy. But the book concludes, not in despair, but on a note of hope. Jehoiachin might be in exile, with the 'good figs' taken away in 597 BC., but he was still king, even if a prisoner. Judeans still reckoned their years from his accession, as was the custom with any reigning monarch. When, an old and broken man, he was released from prison by one of Nebuchadnezzar's weakling successors and restored to a royal position in exile (31–33), it mattered little to history; but it was a sign to the other exiles that the new day was about to dawn. Jehoiachin himself did not apparently live to see the return, but it seems likely that his descendants did. Verse 34 has received archaeological confirmation of a most unusual type, for a cuneiform tablet which was virtually Jehoiachin's 'Ration Card' has been discovered. So the book ends on a note of peace and quiet expectation: God's plan will yet be fulfilled.

TO THINK ABOUT: What was the point in detailing all these captured temple vessels (Ezra 8:24–30)? Why was it important to the Judeans that the temple vessels should be finally returned? If the false prophets foretold this too (28:3), why are they condemned as 'false'? How does the New Testament re-interpret the 'sacred vessels of the Lord'? What is the value of the little footnote about King Jehoiachin (compare 2 Kings 25:27–30)?